TEXT: Jesús Bermúdez López
  Jefe de la Sección de Promoción Cultural
  del Patronato de la Alhambra y Generalife

  Pedro Galera Andreu
  Catedrático de Historia del Arte
  de la Universidad de Jaén

© ALL RIGHTS RESERVED
© COPYRIGHT:
  Patronato de la Alhambra y Generalife
  Editorial Comares

PLANS & DRAWINGS: Sección de Mapas, Planos y Dibujos
  del Archivo del Patronato de la Alhambra y Generalife.
  Manuel López Reche & Abelardo Alfonso Gallardo
  Servicio de Conservación del Patronato de la Alhambra y Generalife

TYPOGRAPHY: Alfonso Meléndez & Andrés Trapiello

TRANSLATION: John Chidley

TRANSLATER'S NOTE: Since most proper, and some common, nouns have been
  left in Spanish the reader might find it useful to remember the meaning of a
  few of them : palacio (palace), puente (bridge), puerta (doorway, gate), sala
  (hall), torre (tower); patio and plaza are now common in English. Other
  words are explained in the text or may be found in the glossary.

PHOTOGRAHS: Valentín García, EXCEPT PHOTOGRAPHS ON PAGES **11**, **26**, **48**, **66**, **73**, **84**,
  90, **101**, **110**, **112**, **123** (above),**134** (below), **135** y **160**: Sección de Fotografías del
  Archivo del Patronato de la Alhambra y Generalife ■ **12**, **18-19**, **21**, **95**, **104**, **123**
  (below), **149**: Archive Editorial Comares ■ Cover, **8**, **10**, **52-53**, **157**, **176-177**:
  Paisajes Españoles ■ **68-69**, **140**: Museo Sorolla, Madrid ■ **13**: Patrimonio
  Histórico-Artístico del Senado (Photograph: Oronoz, Madrid) ■ **91**: Colección
  Fundación Gala-Salvador Dalí, Figueres (Gerona) ■ **122**: Bayerische Staats-
  gemäldesammlungen. München ■ **137**: Private collection (Goyo Fotocolor,
  Granada) ■ **144**: Museum Für Islamische Kunst. Staatliche Museen Zu Berlin.
  Preussischer Kulturbesitz ■ **168**: Asociación Cultural Granada Artística (Goyo
  Fotocolor, Granada) ■ **171**: Private collection (Photograph: Gonzalo de la Serna,
  Madrid)

PRODUCTION: Miguel Ángel del Arco Torres, Mario Fernández Ayudarte & Servicios
  Técnicos del Patronato de la Alhambra

PRINTING: Copartgraf S.C.A.

BINDING: Comares, S.L.

ISBN: 84-8151-831-X · COPYRIGHT DEPOSIT: GR.-306-1999 · PRINTED IN SPAIN

Preface

Access to the Alhambra

Visiting the Alhambra **36**

La Alcazaba

The Charles V Palace and environs

The Nasrid Palaces

The Generalife

The Environs of the Alhambra

LIST OF PLANS AND DRAWINGS

▲ An aerial view
of the Alhambra, built on
the Sabika hill, a foothill
of Sierra Nevada above
the Vega of Granada

Preface

The Alhambra: situation and history

THE ALHAMBRA sits atop the Sabika hill, last bastion of the mountains of Sierra Nevada, which penetrates the interior of a fertile vega or plain between the rivers Darro and Genil. Facing her is the Albayzín and the Sacromonte. A Muslim poet described the hill as a crown and the Alhambra as a great ruby set in it.

In our own time it has been compared to 'a boat anchored between the mountains and the plain'. Like an acropolis, it dominates the city of Granada.

References to buildings in the Alhambra date back to the 9th century, but there must already have existed Roman, or earlier, constructions. After the civil war or fitna which followed the fall of the Caliphate of Cordova in the 11th century, the capital of the then Cora or province of Granada was moved with its Taifa kingdom of the Zirids from Elvira to Granada and a court was set up in a fortress in the Albayzín. From ancient times **9** its slopes had been populated with the nucleus of a vigo-

rous community, mostly Jewish, vital in the development of the city of Granada.

▲ From the top of the hill the Alhambra presides, like an acropolis, over the city of Granada below

At that time the sultan's 'prime minister', Samuel B. Nagrella (993-1055) rebuilding on abandoned ruins, constructed his palace on the Sabika hill.

The Almoravid and Almohad invasions from North Africa in the 12th century led to several tumults in the Albayzín fortress and the Alhambra buildings, the latter serving as a refuge, sometimes for the local Andalusian parties and at others for the North African invaders.

Al-Ahmar (1232-1273), founder of the Nasrid dynasty, at first installed himself in the old Albayzín fortress but quickly noted the attractions of the ruined site on the Sabika **10** hill and decided to move his seat and court there. This was the beginning of the Alhambra that we know today.

The Nasrid sultanate of Granada (1232-1492) was the last Islamic state in the Iberian peninsula. Al-Ahmar, descendent of a tribe of Arabic origin governing in Arjona (Jaén), created a sultanate which encompassed the Mediterranean coast from Tarifa to beyond Almería and, inland, part of the present province of Jaén.

Under political pressure of all sorts, Islamic and Christian; from North Africa or neighbouring Christian kingdoms; Granada survived for 260 years only by clever diplomacy, changing its relations and alliances as circumstances dictated. The break-up of the Almohad empire around 1228, in what is sometimes called a second fitna or civil war, had greatly benefited the Nasrids, leaving them

▼ Detail of the background from the painted panel 'Virgin & Child', showing Granada (c. 1500). Mateu Collection.

with the extensive territory mentioned above and as the only inheritors of the mantle of Islam in the Peninsula.

Internally however, the situation was by no means stable. Risings by local governors, as well as dynastic and palace intrigues were a constant threat as a glance at the **11** list of ruling sultans, some of them assassinated, others dethroned and sometimes later reinstated, shows only too well.

By the end of the first half of the 14th century, Granada could no longer count on the support of the Merinids of Morocco and so sought it from the Turks at the

▼ A mapa mundi of the known world in 1439. On the left, with shaded background, is the sultanate of Granada. Facsimile in the Naval Museum, Madrid.

other end of the Mediterranean. The loss, in 1462, of Gibraltar (a vital link with North Africa) and the ever increasing tributes demanded by the Christians, mark the Nasrid decline.

12 From 1481 onwards, sultan Muley Abu-l-Hasan Ali, campaigned with some success, but the discontent of his

▲ Representation by Francisco Pradilla (1882) of the surrender by Boabdil of the keys of Granada to the Catholic Monarchs.

people and rebellions forced him to devolve power to his viziers (ministers). Meanwhile his wife and Christian concubine were fighting over the respective rights to the throne of their sons, a battle finally won for Abu Abd Allah (Boabdil), son of the former. During a military expedition he was captured by the Christians and released only after a substantial ransom had been paid and, more importantly, he had acknowledged certain rights over Granada claimed by the Catholic Monarchs.

Back in power, Boabdil was unable to sustain the kingdom and one by one his cities fell to the Christians: Alhama, Ronda, Loja, Malaga, Baza and Almeria; at last leaving only Granada, over populated with refugees and under siege. Accepting the inevitable, the city was surrendered on 2nd January 1492 but with conditions —las Capitulaciones— which guaranteed the muslims freedom to practice their religion and preserve their language, justice system and traditions.

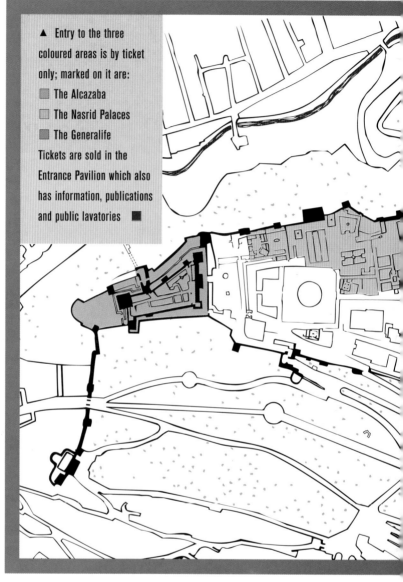

A Palatine City

The Alhambra was a palatine city conceived and built for use of its officials and workforce. Its
14 urban structure, inherited from the purest Hispano-Islamic tradition, evolved over the two and a half cent-

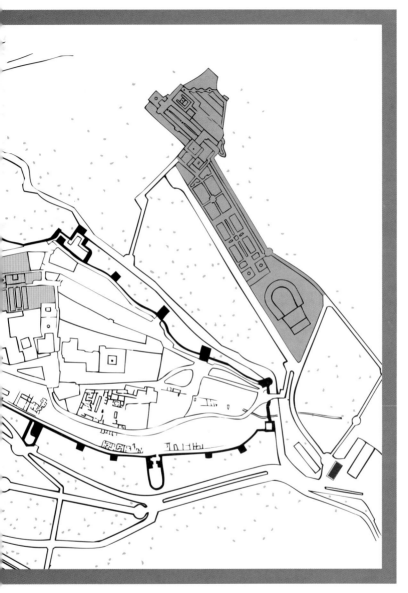

uries of its existence with the logical adaptations demanded by its historical development.

A military precinct or fortress, the Alcazaba, guaranteed, with an elite guard, the internal security of the sultan, his family and government institutions. It was at the **15**
same time a self contained fortified town, strategically

situated at the western extreme of the precinct and connected directly with the rest of the Alhambra.

Separated from the Alcazaba and stretching along the north side, was a **palace complex** reserved for the use of the sultan and his closest family. It contained administration offices arranged according to a protocol that meant entry to successive offices became more and more restricted and privileged. There were also rooms for ministers' meetings and public audiences.

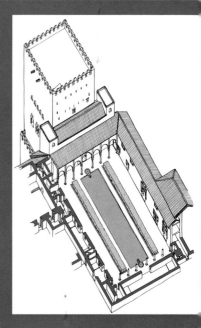

There were several palaces in the complex, built at different times, sometimes starting from scratch and at others adapting and re-decorating

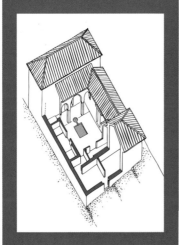

◄▲ Domestic areas in the Alhambra have a similar structure no matter how big or small, or important, they are, for example; the Comares Palace (above) and an idealized reconstruction of a house in the Alhambra Medina (left)

existing buildings. Giving access to the palaces was a street which also separated and distanced them from the rest of the Alhambra.

The palaces have the same layout as any aristocratic

house, but on a grander scale and with a richness of decoration befitting the status of their occupants; and all set between courtyards and gardens in which water and vegetation played an essential role. Each palace had its own bath as well as small oratories where the prescribed prayers could be said throughout the day.

And finally, to serve the needs of this Court, was the **Medina**, a complete town designed for any necessity. Arranged about a main street which gently climbs from west to east, the **Medina** contained a public bath, a mosque and small businesses. Alongside the mosque was the Rauda or cemetary of the sultans and perhaps a Madraza or college. The **Wine Gate** served as principal entrance to the lower zone which contained houses, some of them large, small cisterns and public open spaces. Towards the middle of the street and on either side are two constructions which may be considered true palaces: the **Palacio de los Abencerrajes** and that which later became the **Convento de San Francisco** and is now the Parador de Turismo.

The upper zone of the city contained a variety of craft and workshops, with potters' and glassmakers' kilns, pumps, a tannery and even a mint. The **Acequia Real** ('Royal Conduit'), also called 'of the Sultan', entered the Alhambra here by an aqueduct and descended parallel to the **Calle Real** ('Royal Street') distributing water to all parts of the precinct by means of a complicated piping system. A maze of backstreets, alleyways and covered passages completed the urban picture.

The whole of the Alhambra is surrounded by unbreachable ramparts which connect with those of the city of Granada. Four principal **gates** open along these walls; two in the north, **The Arms Gate** and that called **del Arrabal**, and two in the south, **The Justice Gate** and **The Gate of the Seven Floors**. Along the inside of the whole length of **17** the wall ran a sunken walkway for the guard which con-

nected different parts of the precinct and served, in times of seige, as a defensive trench.

There are more than thirty towers distributed along the walls. Some of them had important living quarters, whilst others were designed as vantage points, and still others as strategic links in the complicated defence system. Every one is different in size and form, giving the monument as a whole its own particular fortress appearance.

The Evolution of the Alhambra

THE ALHAMBRA seen today was not built in one go at a determined date. Apart from the amplifications made by the Nasrids in their day which constitute the most important part, there are earlier constructions as well as the important additions and modifications of Christian times which have continued up to our own time. In chronological order, we have then:

◄ The Alcazaba, a fortress independent of the rest of the Ahambra. The interior is a miniature town in which the élite guard of the sultan was based

1. La Alcazaba (Fortress) Possibly the area with the earliest recorded history. Its situation on the top of the hill makes it a perfect vantage for observation and vigilance over the greater part of its surrounds. Its triangular

▲ The Alcazaba is on the highest part of the hill and that with the longest history. The Nasrids added the great towers to 11th century buildings. In the foreground, the walls of Granada, also 11th century

ground plan derives from constructions of the 11th century when the inner walls on the north were built as well as the gateway to the upper level. In the 12th century, the Almoravids did some building work and adaptation.

2. The Fortified Alhambra From the 13th century onwards the Nasrids gave the **Alcazaba** its present form and structure by building the great towers

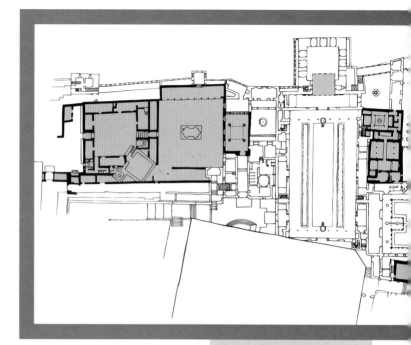

and the whole precinct was framed within another, with a walkway for the guard and the important entrance which is

► Court of the Myrtles the main axis of the Comares Palace, dominated by the great tower. Inside is the Throne Room

the the **Arms Gate**. From then began the enclosure and fortification of the whole monument with its walls and, added at intervals, towers and gates.

3. The First Palaces Once the circling walls defined the enclosed area the first palaces were built. Apart from that of Ismail, of which only vestiges remain, the Pórtico del Partal is the earliest surviving Nasrid palace.

4. The Comares Palace This was built, partly on older remains, during the sultanate of Yusuf I (1333-54) who **22** didn't live to see it finished. To this sultan, a great builder, we also owe **The Justice Gate** and **The Gate of the**

◄ Overall plan of the Nasrid Palaces in the Alhambra. The coloured areas are the oldest parts

Seven Floors. Also from the first half of the 14th century are the Mosque, the Rauda ('cemetary'), the palace in the **Convento de San Francisco** and the **Palacio de los Abencerrajes**.

▲ The cruciform Court of the Lions; in the middle is the famous fountain which gives it its name

5. The Palace of the Lions This was built in the latter half of the 14th century during the second part of the divided reign of Muhammad V (1362-1391), the most brilliant period of Nasrid architecture in the Alhambra. The greater part of the redecoration of other buildings in the

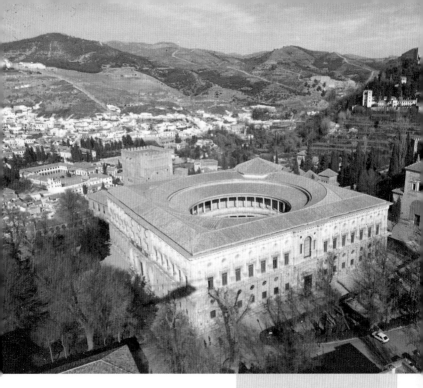

monument is also due to this sultan.

6. The Christian Alhambra
The last and most radical changes to the Alhambra occurred after the Christian conquest. New concepts led to the modification of buildings and urban structure for new uses. The most important of these was the building of **The Charles V Palace**, which, al-

though never completed, added a body to the whole monument which came to be considered as the 'new' Royal House as opposed to the 'old' or Islamic one.

In the 16th century a curtain wall, with the **Torre del Cubo** ('bucket'), was added to the **Alcazaba** and, at its foot, **26** the great cistern of the conde de Tendilla, first Captain-General of the Kingdom of Granada. In the 17th century

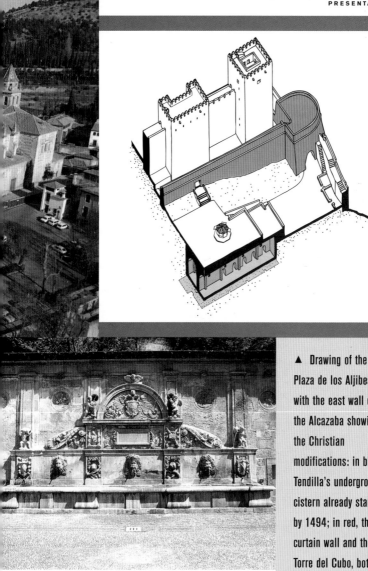

▲ Drawing of the Plaza de los Aljibes with the east wall of the Alcazaba showing the Christian modifications: in blue, Tendilla's underground cistern already started by 1494; in red, the curtain wall and the Torre del Cubo, both added in the 16th century

a garden, the **Jardin de los Adarves**, was planted between the southern walls.

The **Patio de Lindaraja**, the **Patio de la Reja**, the **Church of Santa María**, the **Convento de San Francisco** and the **Fountain of Charles V** are just some of the elements which make up the architectural richness of the **27** Alhambra.

Access to the Alhambra

Pedestrian access

There are three pedestrian routes linking the Alhambra with Granada and its historic quarters.

Cuesta de Gomérez

This starts on the south side of **Plaza Nueva** at the foot of the prow of this so-called 'anchored boat' which is the Alhambra. It is the commonest route with the

▲ The Puerta de las Granadas, built by Pedro Machuca about 1536, introduces the visitor as a triumphal arch, to the Alhambra through the Wood formerly known as 'of the poplars'

following distances from its starting point: to the **Entrance Pavilion**, 1,131 mts.; to The **Wine Gate** inside the monument, 747 mts.; and to the **Centro Cultural Manuel de Falla** and the Carmen de los Martires, 838 mts.

The street is named after a family of North African origin which, according to Luis del Mármol (1520-1600) had its seat in this neighbourhood. In medieval times it was a gully separating the Sabika Hill (on which sits the Alhambra) from the Mauror Hill, crowned by The **Vermilion Towers** (see pp.178–179). These two buildings were connected by a wall which even today serves to define the limits of the city of Granada and the Alhambra precinct. For this reason the **Puerta de las Granadas** was opened in the wall about 1536 as a grand entrance arch. It was designed by Pedro Machuca, the architect of the **Charles V Palace** and like the palace, is built with hewn stone blocks very much in the Italian 'rusticated' style. In the tympanum are the imperial arms supported by Peace and Plenty, with the pomegranates which give the gate its name, on top. This renaissance gate replaced an Islamic one, the remains of which are visible on the right. Behind the gate extends the **Alhambra wood**, crossed by two paths and a road. Of the two footpaths on either side, the one on the right leads to The **Vermilion Towers**, the **Manuel de Falla Auditorium** and the **Carmen de los Mártires**; that on the left, formerly described as 'paved', and which starts from a devotional marble cross of 1641, follows the south flank of the Alhambra walls. The central road, the only one on which traffic is allowed, goes through the middle of the wood, a veritable nature heritage site with centenarian elms, horse chestnuts, oaks and more. In the 18th century this wood was known as 'of the poplars'. Half way up the road is the **Puerta de Bib-Rambla** ('of a sandy river esplanade', also known as the 'Arch of the Ears') originally in the central town square of the same name. It was demolished at the end of the 19th **29** century and reconstructed here in 1935. At the top of

► General plan of approaches from the city: 1. Plaza Nueva; 2. Puerta de las Granadas; 3. Vermilion Towers; 4. Auditorio y Centro Cultural Manuel de Falla; 5. Carmen de los Mártires; 6. Puerta de Bib-Rambla; 7. Monument to Ángel Ganivet; 8. Plaza del Realejo; 9. Pilar del Realejo; 10. Cruz de los Mártires; 11. Paseo de los Tristes; 12. Puente del Aljibillo; 13. Puerta de Hierro

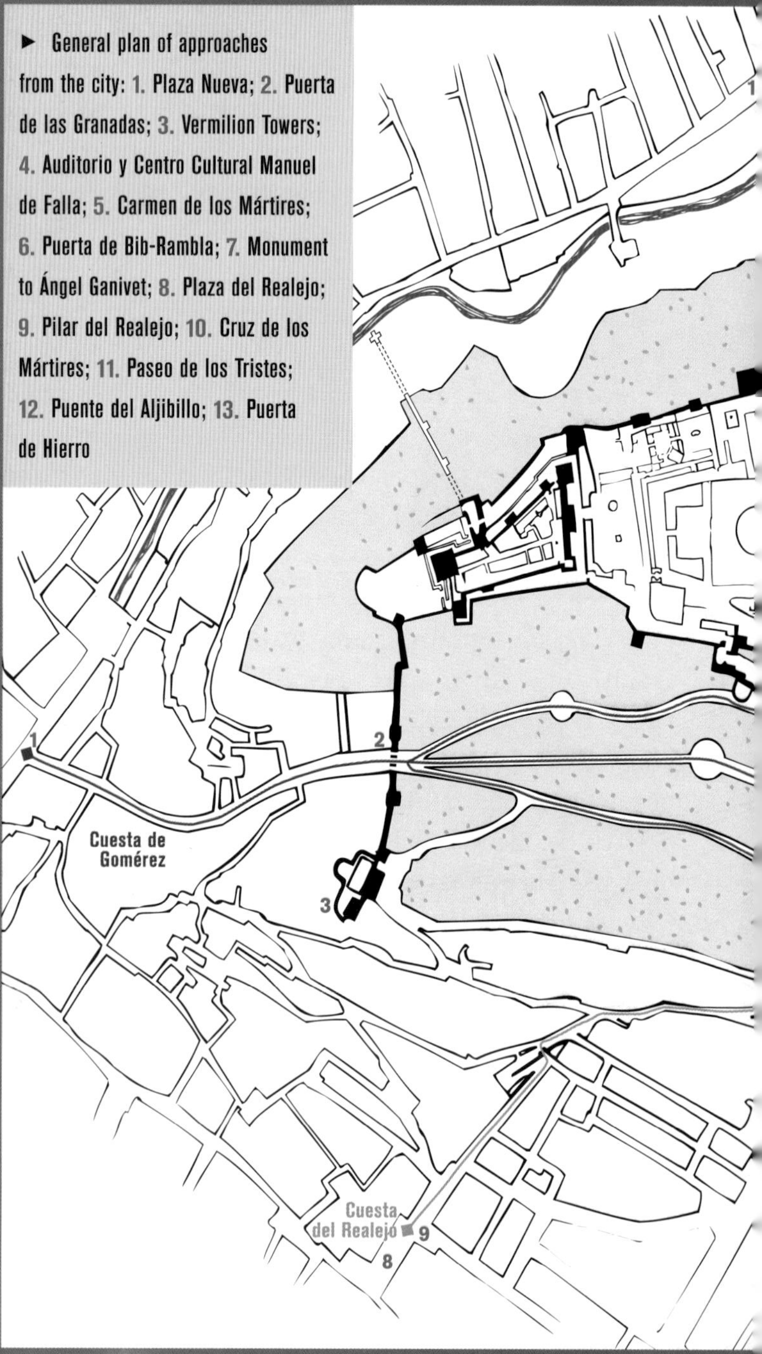

Cuesta de Gomérez

Cuesta del Realejo

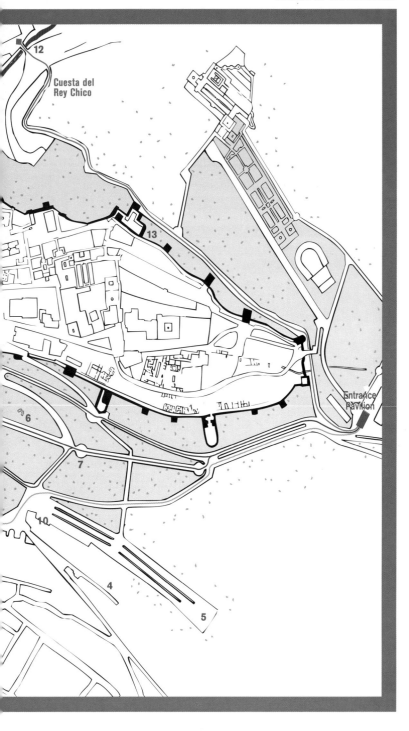

12

Cuesta del
Rey Chico

13

Entrance
Pavilion

6

7

10

4

5

the road is a monument by Juan Cristóbal erected in 1921 as a memorial to Angel Ganivet (1865-1898) the Granadine man of letters.

▲ The begining of the Cuesta del Realejo, the principal route from this district to the Alhambra. On the left, the Fountain of the same name

Cuesta del Realejo

Perhaps the shortest route up but also the steepest of the three. Distances from the start are as follows: to the **Entrance Pavilion**, 874 mts.; to the **Wine Gate** inside the monument, 766 mts.; to the **Centro Cultural Manuel de Falla** and the **Carmen de los Mártires**, 447 mts. It sets off from the Realejo quarter, one of the most typical of Granada, where the Nasrid sultans came to relax in the royal orchards and vegetable gardens. The Bab al-Fajjarin or 'Gate of the Potters', gave access to the quarter as well as its name. Alongside is the Realejo plaza, formerly called 'Upper Realejo'.

The **Realejo route** starts off alongside a stone fountain

of 1616, restored in the 19th century, and ascends between numerous carmens reminiscent of those of the Albayzín. At the end of the climb stands the principal tower of the Hotel Alambra Palace, a 'neo-arabic' building of 1910. The path terminates in the **Peña Partida**, alongside the **Paseo de los Mártires** and el Mauror, a wide, open space on the south side of the Alhambra walls, formerly called 'Alhabul', where there were numerous underground dungeons and where the Catholic Monarchs, Ferdinand and Isabella (1474-1504) built a hermitage dedicated to the holy martyrs. Today the area is home to several cultural institutions and organizations. At the start is the cross erected in 1901 as a menorial to Christian captives.

▶ The Cuesta del Rey Chico, one of three approaches to the Alhambra from Granada and the most direct connection with the Albayzín and the Sacromonte; in the background the Torre de la Cautiva

Cuesta del Rey Chico

Of the three routes this is the nearest to the Albayzín and the Sacromonte. Distances from the start are as **33** follows: to the **Entrance Pavilion**, 785 mts.; to the **Wine**

Gate inside the monument, 1,393 mts.; to the **Centro Cultural Manuel de Falla** and the **Carmen de los Mártires**, 1,224 mts. It starts off alongside the river Darro, at the end of the **Paseo de los Tristes** ('of the mourners'), dominated by the impressive walls of the Alhambra.

It owes its name to a famous legend according to which Aixa, Boabdil's mother (Boabdil was el 'Rey Chico', the 'Little King') helped her son escape from the Alhambra and his father to put himself at the head of the rebels who had occupied the Albayzín opposite. This cuesta has received many other names. The most traditional was 'of the mills' as this was the name given to the gully separating the hillsides of the Generalife and the Alhambra. In the lower part were several water-mills of which some remains are still to be seen, together with conduits and aqueducts leading to the centre of town. It was also called, at the end of the 19th century, 'of the dead', because it was from here that the funeral cortèges processed up to the cemetery behind the Alhambra. At the beginning of this century it was called 'of the cobbles' from the cobbling of the first stretch.

It starts off from the **Puente del Aljibillo** and after the first steep climb leaves the city behind by entering the gully. On the right are the walls and towers of the monument, dominated by the **Torre de las Damas** ('of the Ladies') and on the left the lower parts of the Generalife gardens. Halfway up on the right is a bastion defending one of the four external gates of the Alhambra, the **Puerta del Arrabal** ('of the outskirts'), which lies at the foot of the **Torre de los Picos** ('spikes'), entry to which was via the **Puerta de Hierro** ('Iron') through a gothic **34** arch bearing the arms of the Catholic Monarchs. In front of these buildings and behind a wrought iron gate, is the original lower entry to the Generalife estate, climbing between the walls of the orchards.

Succeeding one another on the way up are the **Torre del Cadí, de la Cautiva, de las Infantas, del Cabo de la Carrera** and **del Agua**, all described in the text. At the end is another former entrance to the Generalife, with a portal bearing the arms of the Granada-Venegas family. Close by is the **Entrance Pavilion** to the whole monument.

Vehicle access

As a consequence of a special planing document for the protection and interior reform of the Alhambra and environs in 1986 and of a subsequent international competition for ideas for arranging the areas around the new approaches to the Alhambra (1988), the whole Monument of the Alhambra and Generalife is now served by a new **access** and a **car park**. This makes communication with the city of Granada and road networks quick and easy.

Public transport An environment-friendly 'train', with separate ticket charges, links the car park with the interior of the monument during opening times.

Apart from licenced city taxis which have several ranks close to entry points, there is a minibus service which connects the monument with the centre of the city, the Albayzín and the Sacromonte, and with a time-table that starts early in the morning and finishes late at night. Information is displayed on the **35** bus stops.

Visiting the Alhambra

There are three official itineraries for visiting the whole Alhambra monument. They are designed to include the three main areas which make it up:

- The Alcazaba
- The Nasrid Palaces
- The Generalife

The three are quite independent and may be visited in any order, but the Patronato de la Alhambra and this guide recommend the following order: Alcazaba-Nasrid Palaces-Generalife.

▲ With the reorganization of the approaches to and intineraries around the Alhambra, a service area has been created known as the Plaza de la Alhambra. In it is the Entrance Pavilion with ticket sales, public lavatories, currency exchange, first aid, audio-visual information, sales of books and in front, models and plans of the Alhambra

Entrance Pavilion

The starting point of the visit is in the **Entrance Pavilion** in the **Plaza de la Alhambra**. To follow the official itineraries it is necessary to go from here to the point where they start, which is the **Wine Gate** in the **Plaza de los Aljibes**. There are two options for getting there; the first is to take the shuttle which links the car park, the **Entrance Pavilion** and the interior of the monument. The second is to take one of the following pedestrian routes which, going by different ways, end at the starting point of the itineraries, the Wine Gate.

a) **Route along the outside of the walls** This follows the southern outside flank of the Alhambra walls and passes through the **Justice Gate.** Distance: 702 mts.; rising and falling ground.

> Car park-path alongside the walls-Tower of the Seven Floors-Torre de las Cabezas-the wood-Justice Gate-Wine Gate.

b) **Route along the inside the walls** (RECOMMENDED). This takes the **Cypress Walk** of the Generalife, and passes through the Upper Alhambra along its **Calle Real**. Distance: 740 mts.; gently rising and falling ground.

> Car park-Cypress Walk-Puente Nuevo-Upper Alhambra-Secano-Calle Real-Wine Gate..

37

Itinerary for Disabled persons

There is a visit, adapted, in so far as is possible in a monument of this sort, for the disabled and which follows in part the official itinerary. Some of the entrances however, are outside the itinerary; information can be obtained at the ticket booths in the **Entrance Pavilion**

Route Outside the Walls

This route along the south flank of the Alhambra walls starts in the south-east corner close to the **Entrance Pavilion** at the point were the **Cuesta del Rey Chico**, a path coming up from the city, terminates.

Gate of the Seven Floors There are several towers along the route outside the walls and the first of the four exterior gates in the precinct; the **Gate of the Seven Floors**. This gate gave entry to the upper ward of the Alhambra Medina. Built in the 14th century on top of an older gate, it was destroyed when Napoleonic troops blew-up this whole section of the walls when they retired from the fortress in 1812. It was rebuilt from 1960 onwards using information from antique prints.

The next two of several towers of different sizes and functions projecting from the walls in this stretch leading to the **Justice Gate** are, the **Torre del Capitán** ('Captain') and the **Torre de la Bruja** ('Witch'), both giving on to the Upper Alhambra or **Medina**.

Torre de las Cabezas Among the towers that project from the walls this ('of the heads'), is one of the largest and has an important bastion added. The space before the walls and towers was not originally covered with trees and shrubs as now, but rather an open ground would have been used for military drills and parades.

During the building of the **Charles V Palace** in the 16th century, a ramp leading to a gate was made to carry up the construction materials in carts and the **Puerta de los Carros** ('carts') is still the only one with vehicle access to the interior of the Alhambra. A few yards further down is one of the principal entrances to the Alhambra.

The Justice Gate and Esplanade This is the most monumental of the four external gates and was built in 1348. Adjoining it is a later bastion to which was added the **Charles V Fountain**, a brilliant work of renaissance art, with mythological reliefs on a

▲ The Justice Gate, one of four external gates in the walls and the most monumental. It was built for Yusuf I in 1348

background now nearly lost and allegorical masks, added in the 17th century, alluding to the three rivers of Granada (Darro, Genil & Beiro).

The **Justice Gate** is also known as 'The Gate of the Esplanade' due to the extensive open ground before it. This gate contains some of the most potent symbols of the Alhambra, such as the hand in the keystone of the outer arch, the fingers of which represent the five fundamental obligations of Islam. A gap left open to the sky for defensive purposes separates this arch from the gate proper with columns engaged in the wall whose capitals **39**

are inscribed with these same obligations. Above the arch are, successively, the symbolic Narid key, a tablet record-
40 ing the gate's construction and finally, higher still, a gothic Virgin and Child, a copy of the original by Roberto

Alemán now in the Fine Arts Museum, proclaims, no less symbolically, the Christian occupation of the Catholic Monarchs. The great door, covered with iron plates, retains its original leaves, locks and bolts and was recently restored. Inside, the path slopes upwards and makes four right-angle turns covered by different ceilings painted with mock bricks in red. At the exit is an altarpiece dating from 1588 and, alongside, a marble tablet inscribed with gothic letters. The inside face of the gate retains some of the rhombic ceramic tiling in the spandrels of the arch.

Leading from the gate is a wide path at the foot of the walls which were reinforced after the conquest with Islamic tombstones. A short climb leaves us at the **Wine Gate**, the start of the official itineraries.

Route inside the Walls

This route crosses the Upper Alhambra, an area of workshops serving the court and today an archaeological site, along the **Calle Real**, the principal street in the **Medina** and finishes at the **41** **Wine Gate**.

It starts in the **Cypress Walk** which forks at the end. Carrying straight on is the itinerary for the Generalife, although, as has been mentioned, the recommended order for the visit is the **Alcazaba** and then the **Nasrid Palaces**. At this point then, we turn left and enter the Alhambra, crossing over the natural gully of the **Cuesta**

▲ The cloister of the former Convento de San Francisco, today Parador Nacional de Turismo, built on top of the remains of a Nasrid palace

del Rey Chico by a modern bridge linking the walls and the Generalife estate.

From here on the route follows the **Acequia Real** or Royal Conduit which supplied water to the Alhambra.

Entry to the Walled Precint of the Alhambra Entry to the Alhambra is across the **Medina**, today a waste area called 'Secano' and in which can be seen, apart from the aqueduct at the start of the **Acequia Real**, remains of buildings —several ceramic kilns, a tannery and diverse houses— along the inside face of the walls and towers.

The 'Secano' Archaeological Walk This walk, with its clipped cypress hedges and arches and surrounding gardens, was designed about 1930 to allow a view of the archaeological remains in the area. In the 19th century a great part of the Alhambra, but not the palaces, was in private hands and contained small carmens; this area is an example.

Beyond the cypress arches, on the right, is the **Convento de San Francisco**, built in the 16th century over the remains of a small Islamic palace and today the Parador de Turismo. On the left looking down, the remains of several Nasrid houses may be seen.

At the end of the walk, standing out among the archaeological remains, is the traditionally named **Palacio de los Abencerrajes**. Archaeological excavations and reconstructions since 1930 have revealed not only the remains of the palace but also two superimposed Islamic baths, a dungeon or store and domestic constructions.

Calle Real of the Alhambra From medieval times this was the principal street of the **Medina**, but the building of the **Convento de San Francisco** and changes made when, in modern times, this was turned into an hotel (the Parador), mean that the street now disappears here.

From further down may be seen the **Wine Gate** in the distance and further still the entrance to the **Alcazaba**. Noteworthy on the way down this stretch are the **Mosque Bath** or **del Polinario** and the **Ángel Barrios Museum**, both being parts of the house where this Granadine musician and composer, a contemporary of Manuel de Falla, lived. The museum is dedicated to Barrios and his artistic and intellectual circles of the first third of the 20th

43

century. It contains a small but important collection of drawings, paintings, watercolours and music scores all dedicated to the musician, who died in 1964, or to his father Antonio, as well as personal effects and correspondence. The museum itself occupies that part of the house which was the now disappeared tavern of Antonio, *el Polinario*, one of the last cicerones of the Alhambra and where intellectuals and artists of the early twentieth century would meet. Famous visitors include Ravel, Strauss, Lorca, the Machado brothers, Zuloaga, Rusiñol, Sargent et. al. Both the bath and the museum may be visited at special times.

Santa María de la Alhambra

This church was built on the site of the Grand Mosque of the Alhambra, demolished in 1576 as ruinous. It was constructed between 1581 and 1618 to designs by Juan de Herrera and Juan de Orea and finished by Ambrosio de Vico at the beginning of the 17th century, although with poorer materials than had originally been envisaged.

◄ Interior of the Church of Santa María de la Alhambra

In plan it is a Latin cross with side chapels. Noteworthy are the baroque retable (1671) of the high altar, and statues of saints Ursula and Susana and a crucifixion all by Alonso de Mena, one of the principal sculptors of Spain's Golden Age. The name of the church is celebrated in a statue of the Virgin, a pietà, by Torcuato Ruiz del Peral of between 1750-60. In Holy Week this statue is carried through the Alhambra woods in a traditional and impressive procession.

The Wine Gate

In many ways this gate continues to serve the function it had during Nasrid times. It is the principal access gate to the **Medina** of the Alhambra and that which, within the whole walled area, encloses off the residential and work-

shop sectors serving the court. Being an internal gate it has no turning, but a straight-through access, unlike the external gates built with bends. Inside, the vaulted ceiling is delicately painted and, still in place, are the benches for the guard. Structurally it is one of the oldest buildings in the Alhambra, being attributed to the time of sultan Muhammad III (1302-1309), although the two decorated façades are of different dates. That on the west side, worked in sandstone, dates from the end of the 13th century or beginning of the 14th, in spite of the fact that the stone tablet above the lintel mentions sultan Muhammad V (mid-fourteenth century). This was the outer face of the gate and so has the traditional key symbol above the keystone to the arch. The eastern or inside façade, although with a similar scheme, was decorated during Muhammad V's second reign (after 1367, the date of the Jaén, Baeza and Ubeda campaigns). Of note are the beautiful spandrels of the arch decorated with tiles of the 'cuerda seca' technique, the stucco compositions which frame the windows and the traces of painting on the right of the arch.

◄ The Wine Gate, the original entrance to the Medina of the Alhambra. Now it is the starting point for the itineraries to the Alcazaba and the Nasrid Palaces. Below right, detail of the delicate decoration of its inner façade

47

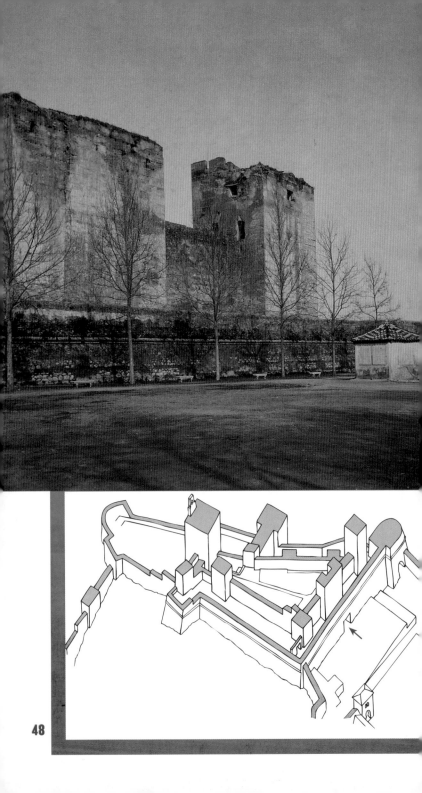

The Alcazaba

Plaza de los Aljibes

Stretching between the **Wine Gate** and the **Alcazaba**, the **Plaza de los Aljibes** ('Cisterns') was formed by filling-in a deep gully which separated the former from the rest of the Alhambra. Underneath is a massive cistern with impressive vaulting built soon after the Christian conquest (work was seen in progress in 1494) by the first governor, the conde de Tendilla after whom it is named. Up to the middle

◄ The Plaza de los Aljibes towards the end of the 19th century. Underneath it is the great 'aljibe' or cistern built for the conde de Tendilla around 1494

◄ Drawing of the Alcazaba

► The Plaza de los Aljibes today. In the middleground on the left is the modern entrance to the Alcazaba

of the twentieth century the plaza extended to the northern walls, but expanding archaeological excavations, started at the beginning of the century, removed the in-filling to leave exposed an important area previously unrecorded.

The Citadel

Properly speaking the **Alcazaba** is a fortified miniature town isolated from the rest of the Alhambra. In plan it is a triangle, the walls marked out with towers, three of which, the **Torre del Adarguero** ('shield bearer'), the **Torre Quebrada** ('broken') and the **Homage Tower** are set in the eastern flank or base of the triangle

▼ The north side of the Alcazaba. The upper walls are of the 11th century. To these the Nasrids added, among others, the outer walls, the Arms gate-tower and, in the distance, the great Watch Tower

facing the **Plaza de los Aljibes**, whilst the imposing **Watch Tower** closes the apex to the west. This Nasrid perimeter sits on top of an older fortress which was reconstructed and enlarged to give a complex pattern of interconnected defensive walls which made it stronger than ever. Entry to the **Alcazaba** is through a large modern door in a curtain wall at the northern end of which is a

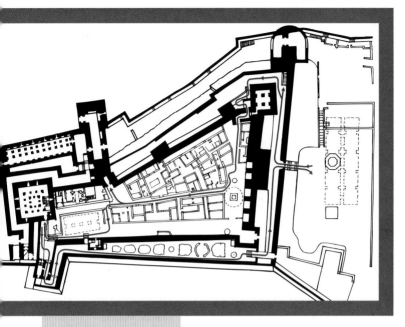

▲ Plan of the Alcazaba with the itinerary marked in red

cylindrical tower called the **Torre del Cubo** ('bucket') built in the 16th century and which has a terrace with magnificent views not to be missed. The visit to the **Alcazaba** continues going round the base of the **Homage Tower**.

The walls which close the north of the **Alcazaba** date to the 11th century when the dynasty of the Zirids ruled in Granada, then a taifa kingdom, and demonstrate the antiquity of the fortress as mentioned above. Along the wall are three small, but stout, towers with a square plan and others similar are found about this interior precinct.

In the 13th century the Nasrids, when reconstructing the fortress, built an enclosing wall around the whole which linked up with the walls of the Alhambra. At the same time, from the flanks of the **Alcazaba**, a wall inter-connected with the defensive walls of the city of Granada; on the north descending to the river Darro to link up with the nearby Albayzín and the Sacromonte; and to the south with the Mauror hill and the **Vermilion Towers**.

51

◄ Aerial view from the west of the Alcazaba with the Watch Tower in front. In the foreground, on the right, can be seen one of the walls connecting the Alhambra with Granada

But probably most impressive in this defence system are the three towers mentioned at the beginning and especially the **Homage Tower**.

The Homage Tower

This is possibly among the earliest of Nasrid buildings
54 and some references suggest that it may have been used as a temporary residence by the first sultan of the dynasty. The

▲ The Homage Tower (on the left) dominates the Alcazaba and environs. In this wood engraving of between1862-1873 by G. Doré, its important role in the defence and control of the precinct can be appreciated

upper storey is laid out with living quarters, a fact which shows that this was, at all events, where the military chief of the Alhambra garrison dwelt.

It is not the tallest of the towers, but the fact that it is built on the most elevated part of the hill, make it the highest over all. This and its position turned slightly out of line with the other towers make it a perfect

55

vantage point. It has five storeys, including a terrace and a basement with what is either a dungeon or store. At its foot is the original entrance to the **Alcazaba**, a simple wall describing a zig-zag passage and which hides the doorway opening in the walls so that it cannot be seen from the outside.

Through the doorway is vaulted passage with more right-angle bends , at one end and before coming out in the **Plaza de Armas**, is a gap opening to the sky for defence and control from above. Two exits lead off from this covered corridor, one to the lower floors and the basement of the **Homage Tower**, and the other climbs to the ramparts and to the same tower.

This was not the only entrance to the **Alcazaba**, but it was perhaps the most important since from here the guard was distributed all over the Alhambra and it connected with the walkway on the outer walls which encircle the **Alcazaba**.

The interior of the Alcazaba

This internal space of the **Alcazaba** is a typical feature of medieval fortresses and known as the **Plaza de Armas** ('of Arms'), open and with hardly any buildings, it was a place to drill the troop in times of peace and a mustering point in times of war. Here however, it was

56 transformed into barracks and service buildings for the elite guard of the

▲ The tower-gateway of Arm is one of the earliest Nasrid buildings in the Alhambra. As the only one of the Alhambra four great gates opening wit the city confines it was the principal connection with Granada.

► The Arms Gate with a do right-angle bend inside direc inherited from Almohad mod The spandrels of the pointed horse-shoe arch retain rema of rich decorative tilework

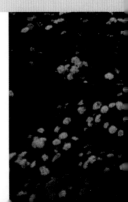

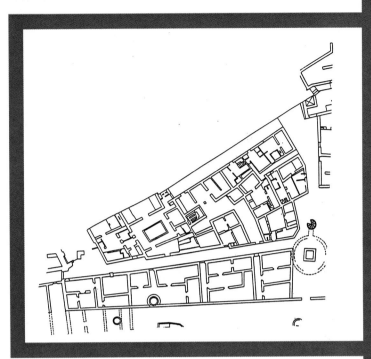

sultan. Known as the **Barrio Castrense**, it is in fact a town in miniature with the same urban structure as any other small Hispano-Islamic town.

A narrow street running east-west along the whole length separates two different blocks. On the north side, huddled together, are the remaining walls and pavements of houses of different sizes but identical structure. On the other side of the street are remains with similar characteristics, but more uniformly laid out and with spacious courtyards, all of which suggests that they were warehouses and/ or barracks for the troops.

Dungeons

There are many of these in the Alhambra, at least
58 twelve have been found to date, three of them in the
Alcazaba. One, as has been mentioned, is beneath the

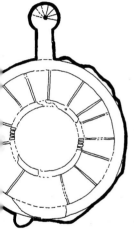

Homage Tower, there is another beneath the **Watch Tower** and the third is alongside the base of the **Broken Tower**. This last is a hollow excavated in the ground and now protected by a parapet and a grille. In the thirties a staircase was built alongside for access.

In general these dungeons were shaped like an upside-down funnel and most of those found in the Alhambra still have the original flooring with cell-like spaces for the prisoners defined by brickwork forming segments in the circular groundplan. These dungeons were also used to store grain, spices or even salt.

The Bath and Cistern

The **Alcazaba**, as with all other residential areas, contained two essentials; a communal bath and a cistern to supply both it and the citadel. The layout typical of these

◄ Plan of the military quarter of the Plaza de Armas in the Alcazaba

▲ Plan and section of the dungeon in the Alcazaba

► Plan of the bath and cistern ▢ ▢

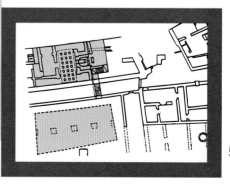

59

buildings can still be seen from above the bath, although it is now ruinous. Entry was through a corridor at the foot of the **Watch Tower**. This led to a disrobing room with further on, on the left, a lavatory and on the right the resting or cool room, followed by the steam room in which may be seen remains of the hypocaust and space for the boiler. At the end is the large storeroom for the firewood.

The cistern, altered in the 16th century, has a double-barrelled vault supported on pillars. Originally it was filled by rainwater but was later connected to the **Acequia Real** by a complicated hydraulic system.

Terrace of the Arms Gate

Giving off the **Barrio Castrense** is a lookout with some of the most spectacular views of the city, the Albayzín and the Sacromonte to be had; this is the terrace of the **Arms Gate**, already so called (Bib Silah) in a document of 1470. This gate is one of the four recognised external entries to the Alhambra and the one normally used in the past by the citizens of Granada to enter the fortress. It is also one of the most important Alhambra buildings of the 13th century and its structure and decoration faithfully reflect the tradition of Almohad gates with a zig-zag passage.

From the terrace the structure and working of the gate

may be seen. The outer western face gives on to the city and the double-bend passage inside ends in a T-junction. One path, going round a long building which were stables, continues below the barbican wall towards the **Watch Tower**. The other leads by a wide and cobbled street, to the interior of the Alhambra.

▲ This engraving by A. Laborde (1812) gives an idea of the historical importance of the Watch Tower, shown here with the original belfry, with respect to the city of Granada and all of its surroundings

The Watch Tower

Without doubt one of the most potent symbols of both the **61** Alhambra and of Granada itself. In fact in 1843 Isabel II

granted the city the right to include its image in the official coat of arms. This massive tower is a landmark from far off, proudly proclaiming, as it were, the presence of the Monument.

▲ The terrace of the Watch Tower is the principal viewpoint of the Alhambra, with magnificent perspectives of the city and countryside round about; the lower city of Granada, the Albayzín, the Sacromote, Sierra Nevada and the Vega

It is however one of the most enigmatic towers in the Alhambra; it is not known, for example, where the original entry was, the present one being a modern adaptation of an opening by the ramparts. It has a basement storey with a separate entrance and a dungeon or grain storeroom. Its total height of almost 30 mts. is divided into four floors of living accommodation which become more spacious the higher the storey. This is because, to ensure stability, the outer walls get thinner and thinner as they rise. The tower was originally topped with high battlements which fell into ruin over the centuries

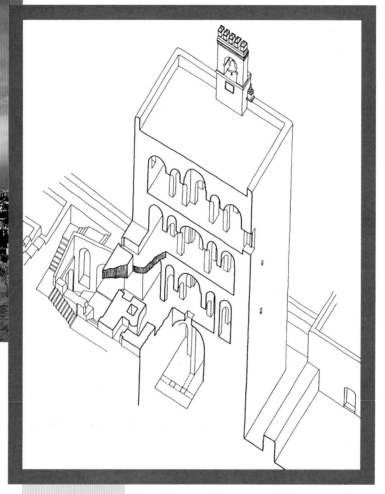

▲ Axonometric
view and section of
the Watch Tower

although some fragments of them may be seen at its foot on the east side. Like other towers it has had several different names; one such, 'Torre del Sol' ('sun') because its shadow marked the hours like a sundial; another name, 'Torre de la Campana' refers to the bell, placed at the beginning of the Christian occupation in the north-east corner, but moved to its present position in 1840. The present belfry is a late 19th century reconstruction. Over its long history the great bell has rung out marking the rhythm of **63** daily life in the city and Vega; the dawn and evening bell, the curfew; as well as anouncing important events.

It is an old-established custom in Granada to climb the tower on 2nd January, the day of the Christian conquest of the city, when anybody can ring the bell. It is said that if any single girl of marriageable age does so, she will be engaged within the year. These customs possibly derive from another tradition; that it was from here the royal standards of the Catholic Monarchs were first flown on this day.

As an extraordinary vantage point with superb all-round views out over the whole city and surrounding countryside, a visit to the top of the tower is not to be missed.

Torre de la Pólvora y Jardín de los Adarves

On the south side of the fortress protecting the **Watch Tower** is the **Torre de la Pólvora** ('gunpowder'). It would also have been of importance in controlling the stretch of wall wich connects up with the Vermilion Towers from here (see pp. 178-179). Now it makes a delightful look-out. On the wall is a stone tablet, placed here in 1957, bearing a well-know

verse by Francisco de Icaza referring to a beggar: 'Give him alms woman, / for nothing in life / is as sad as being blind in Granada'.

The **Jardin de los Adarves** ('Ramparts Garden') was formed in the 17th century by filling in the space between the two southern walls of the fortress up to the height of the outer rampart (hence the name). Conceived by the marqués de Mondéjar as a renaissance *belvedere*, it is a possible inspiration for the typical **65**

Granadine carmen of the 19th century and contrasts with the intimate, inward-looking Islamic garden.

The garden is closed off at each end with small towers projecting from the inner wall. Two renaissance-inspired fountains emphasize its Italianate character. In the middle of the garden is a marble fountain, which from 1624 to 1954, was placed on top of the basin of the famous **Fountain of the Lions** and which, according to tradition, was originally in the now disappeared bath of the **Palace of the Lions**.

▲ The fountain now in the Jardin de los Adarves used to be on top of the Fountain of the Lions, as this 19th century photograph (one of the oldest preserved in the Alhambra) shows

From this enchanting spot we leave the **Alcazaba** and crossing the **Plaza de los Aljibes** pass once again through the **Wine Gate** to continue the itinerary which takes us to the entrance to the **Nasrid Palaces**. At this point a visit to the museums in the **Charles V Palace** is possible (but remember to check the entry time-slot for the **Nasrid Palaces** allotted you on your ticket).

▲ In this painting of the Jardin de los Adarves (1917), Joaquin Sorolla neatly captures the 19th century atmosphere of a typical Granadine Carmen

The Charles V Palace and Environs

Through the **Wine Gate** are esplanades in front of the **Charles V Palace** traditionally called **Las Placetas** and which according to the renaissance plan would have been a colonnaded parade ground, but which was never built. The view looking north from here to the Albayzín and the Sacromonte is very picturesque. A low parapet wall closes of this area and allows a view over a paved plaza below with archaeological remains. It was from this plaza that the sultan's subjects climbing up from Granada would continue either to the **Medina** by a path up to the **Wine Gate** or go straight into the **Mexuar** across two stepped courtyards. The first of these is the **Patio de la Madraza** so called because in plan, decoration and structure it is similar to the Madraza (college) in the city. The second is known as the **Patio de Machuca** after the architect of the **Charles V Palace**, who lodged there. In its centre is a Roman style pond. To the north is a reconstructed Nasrid colonnade which would have had its opposite on the south, now marked by an arcade of cypresses.

The Charles V Palace

The presence of a renaissance palace in the heart of the Alhambra, '… like a meteorite stuck in by chance' in the words of Manfredo Tafuri, never fails to surprise by its radical and

▲ A great colonnade was planned for the esplanade in front of the principal façade of the Charles V Palace, but it was never built and little by little the area was turned into gardens, giving today's 'placetas'

almost arrogant rupture with the pre-existing architecture and surroundings. It is however, a jewel of its type, unique among Spanish royal residences and an outstanding work of the Spanish renaissance. To understand the palace it should be looked at not so much as a mansion in a strict sense, but rather as an expression of Empire; reflecting triumphant universal order and Christian unity, personified by Charles V, who chose the site for its symbolism as the last Islamic stronghold in the West.

The original plan, a circle inscribed within a square, reflects the two symbols of earth and heaven united which, although there are precedents in Italy,

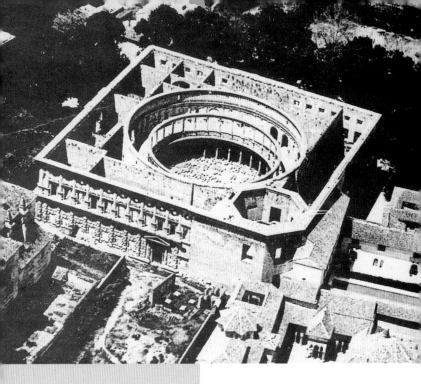

▲ An aerial photograph, taken about 1920, showing the abandoned and roofless state of the Charles V Palace when work stopped after the rebellion of the moriscos in 1568

◄ The gallery of the renaissance palace is a circle, inscribed, with high symbolic meaning, within the square of the façades and wings

is unique in Spain. The design dates from 1526 and is attributed to Pedro Machuca, although he may have copied Italian models and ideas. He directed the work until his death in 1550, when his son Luis took over. The building was largely paid for by taxing the morisco community and their rebellion in 1568 effectively stopped work. So it was that until 1923 all that had been finished were the structural walls, the courtyard, the chapel and the façades, but not, for example the roof. It was Leopoldo Torres Balbás who, from this date, started the programme to complete the work which continues to **73** this day.

▲ Portal of the principal front of the
Charles V Palace in an unfinished oil
painting attributed to Santiago Rusiñol and
now in the Angel Barrios Museum of the
Alhambra

Of note in the palace are: the dignified and elegant circular courtyard with surrounding stone vaulted gallery; the octagonal chapel in the north east corner, a copy of the one at Aquisgran built by Charlemagne, Charles V's ancestor; and above all the two principal façades, that of the west side ('of the Emperor'), with a triumphal portal in severe Doric order above a frieze of military victories in the socles and that of the south side ('of the Empress'), in Ionic order with allegories of fertility and mythological scenes. The treatment of the walls with rusticated pillow-shaped stones, the round windows of the mezzanine and the elegant pedimented windows of the upper storey all clearly evoke the Italian architecture of the circle of Raphael.

► Detail of one of the reliefs carved with battle scenes on the façades of the palace

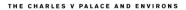

Museums and Exhibition Rooms in the Palace

There are two museums and a permanent Introductory Exhibition to the Alhambra within the **Palace of Charles V** which complete the visit for those who wish to know more about the monument.

The Alhambra Museum This was founded in 1942 as the Museo Arqueológico, the name being changed in 1962 to Museo Nacional de Arte Hispano-Musulman and changed yet again in 1992 to the present one, when its administration passed to the Patronato de la Alhambra. It contains the best collection in the world of Nasrid art, most of the pieces coming from excavations and restorations in the Alhambra itself. It also contains a select and complementary collection of non-Nasrid Islamic artefacts giving a fuller picture of Al-Andalus and the rest of the Islamic world.

◄ The portal on the south ('Empress') façade of the palace in the Ionic order and with mythological scenes and allegories of fertility

Since 1995 the Museum has been housed in the ground floor of the palace, the refurbishing project receiving the Premio

77

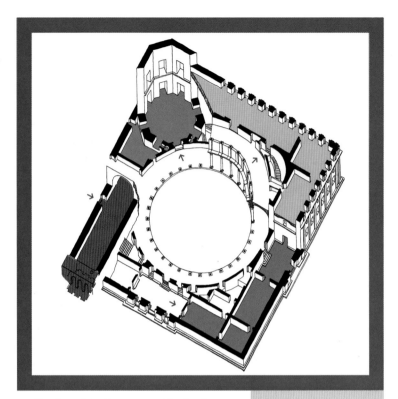

Nacional de Restauración in the same year. The museum was previously housed in the upper floors of the **Nasrid Palaces** attached; these are now used as storerooms and may be visited by researchers.

The Fine Arts Museum This is in the upper floors of the palace which were refurbished to house the museum between 1941 and 1956. The basis of this collection, as with the majority of these museums are the objects confiscated with the suppression of church property in the last century and amplified with donations, acquisitions and loans. Central to the collection are the Granadine paintings and sculptures of the 16th to 20th centuries, particularly those of the so-called 'Granadine School' one of the most important during

▲ One of the rooms in the Alhambra Museum showing two of its most important exhibits; the Gazelles Jar and the door from the Sala de dos Hermanas

▲ The 'Chimneypiece' room in the Provincial Fine Arts Museum

Spain's Golden Age. It is administered by the Consejería de Cultura de la Junta de Andalucía and has guide books available.

Introductory Exhibition to the Monument This was opened in 1992 in a semi-basement opposite the **Mexuar** with a permanent exhibition which seeks to offer the visitor an introductory understanding of the whole Monument of the Alhambra. There are four parts which may be visited in any order and contain models, information panels, exhibition cases and a small video projection room. Opening times are the same as those of the the rest of the monument and entry free, although there **79** may be restrictions at peak times.

The Nasrid Palaces

El Mexuar

The traditional visitors' entrance to the **Nasrid Palaces** was through the **Mexuar**

◄ Portal of the entrance to the Mexuar, start of the visit to the Nasrid Palaces

and perhaps because of this it has suffered a great number of reforms, starting in Nasrid times. This makes interpreting and understanding the building difficult.

El **Mexuar** (Ar. *Maswar*) was where the Sura or council of ministers held their meetings, but it also served as a waiting area or ante-chamber when the sultan gave audience.

Entrance Front

This has not preserved characteristic Nasrid proportions and although it contains elements from that period, these have been incorporated from elsewhere. It is now thought to have been built in Christian times.

The arrocabe or wooden tablet with an inscription preserves the original text for the front although it must have been in a different place: 'Oh foundation of the lofty

▲ The itinerary of the Nasrid Palaces:
1. Mexuar; 2. Oratory; 3. Patio del
Cuarto Dorado; 4. Façade of the
Comares Palace; 5. Court of the
Myrtles; 6. Palace Dwellings; 7. Sala de
la Barca; 8. Palace lavatory; 9. Comares
Hall; 10. Original entrance to the Bath;
11. Present entrance to the Palace of the
Lions; 12. Court and Fountain of the
Lions; 13. Sala de los Mocárabes;
14. Sala de Abencerrajes; 15. Sala de
los Reyes; 16. Sala de Dos Hermanas;
17. Sala de los Ajimeces; 18. Mirador
de Lindaraja; 19. Emperor's Chambers;
20. Peinador de la Reina; 21. Patio de
la Reja; 22. Patio de Lindaraja

► Axonometric view of the
palaces of Comares and of
the Lions:
1. Sala del Mexuar
2. Comares Façade
3. Court of the Myrtles
4. Comares basement
5. Comares Bath
6. Court of the Lions
7. Basement of the Palace
of the Lions

kingdom / showpiece of marvellous workmanship! / You have been opened and, oh, would that it were for a clear victory / and for the beauty of the craftsmanship and for the craftsman who made you: / a monument to the Imam Muhammad. / May the shadow of the most High [be] over all' (from Sp. trans. by A.R. NYKL, 1936-1939).

Interior

The hall of the **Mexuar**, a rectangle, must once have been part of a building pre-dating the **Comares Palace** and the **Palace of the Lions** and was probably built for Ismail I (1314-1325) although it has suffered many alterations. The decoration was modified by Yusuf I (1333-1354) and later by Muhammad V

▲ Photograph of the interior of the Mexuar at the end of the 19th century in which can be seen the separation of the northern end for its use as the chapel choir

(1362-1391) during the second part of his divided reign.

It originally had a central lantern ceiling for overhead lighting but only the four columns and the entablature now remain. In the 16th century the whole area was altered to convert it into a chapel with an upper floor. A wall with a courtyard beyond closed off the hall along the line now taken by the renaissance balustrade. When the wall was demolished the space gained was used as a choir. Noteworthy among the radical alterations to the building are the morisco decorated wooden ceilings and the curious epigraphic stucco frieze which runs along the top of the dado of ceramic tiling. This frieze was brought here from the disappeared portico of the Patio de Machuca and put in place by morisco craftsmen and, reflecting as the text does, the liturgy of the mass, with clear symbolic intent:

'The Kingdom is of God.
Power is of God.
Glory is of God'.

Also noteworthy are the four columns of a type that, **85** with variations, abound in the Alhambra and Nasrid

Granada. They are characterized by slim marble shafts topped by a series of mouldings which form a collar underneath the capital itself. Inspired by Almohad models the capitals are in two parts; the lower cylindrical; the upper cubic and containing the most varied combinations of ornamental motifs. Those in the **Mexuar** preserve, moreover, the original multicolouring.

Another essential element in a Granadine interior is the dado which runs right round the room and is covered with glazed ceramic tiles which make up polygonal figures of stars. The greater part of this dado was brought here to decorate the chapel in the 16th century from the now disappeared southern hall of the **Comares Palace**. This is why some of the centre pieces of the stars bearing the Nasrid arms were replaced by those of the emperor or the Mondéjar family, the three alternating as symbols of power. Some of the original **86** panels were preserved and are now in the **Alhambra Museum**.

▲ Interior of the Mexuar today

◀ Axonometric view of part of the Mexuar oratory.

The Oratory

At the far end of the hall is an oratory, one of several in the Alhambra. The original entrance was via the **Patio de Machuca**. The floor level has been lowered for easier access, but was originally at the level of the small bench beside the windows. This allowed the believer, sitting cross-legged on the floor with an arm resting on the low parapet, to contemplate the landscape and meditate on nature and the power of Allah.

Patio del Cuarto Dorado

Situated between the **Mexuar** and the **Comares Palace**, this patio was where the sultan would give audience to his subjects. It has been much altered over the years and in the 16th century some of the rooms giving on to it were adapted for residential use for the emperor Charles V and his court. Of note here is the arcade on the north side with fretted stucco panels, a foretaste of those in the Comares Palace and which is supported by two of the oldest capitals (12th or 13th century) in the Alambra. These are of a style anterior to the typical Nasrid capital already seen in the **Mexuar**.

The fountain is a copy of that in the **Jardín de Lindaraja** and similar to an original now lost but described by Luis de Mármol in 1600 as, 'a shallow basin in the African fashion, very large, all of a piece and carved as a shell'.

Behind the northern triple-arched arcade is the **Cuarto Dorado** ('Gilded Room'), originally decorated by Muhammad V. It is so called after the beautiful wooden ceiling redecorated and gilded in the time of the Catholic Monarchs, like everything here, as is shown by the presence of their emblematic badges, the yoke and sheaf of arrows. This room would have been used by the officials and secretaries of the Muslim court to record and execute the rulings of the sultan.

◄ Detail of one of the dados with ceramic tiling. The geometric composition starts with a central star or Sino and expands with a succession of new stars

◄ One of the most characteristic features of Nasrid architecture is the cubic capital and there are a great number in the Alhambra varying in size and decorative motifs. This one in the Mexuar preserves much of its original rich colouring

▲ Detail of the decorative wooden ceiling in the Cuarto Dorado, redecorated in the time of the Catholic Monarchs as is shown by the presence of their badges, the yoke and the sheaf of arrows.

► Painting by Mariano Fortuny entitled 'Tribunal in the Alhambra' (1871). Very much influenced by the orientalism of the day and convincingly set in the Patio of the Cuarto Dorado.

Running underneath is the walkway used by the sultan's personal guard. Originally it would have been open and on top of the wall, but the alterations and enlargements which so be-devil interpretation of this part of the Alhambra have left it too, hidden.

The Comares Palace

The Palace Façade

The façade rises majestically opposite the portico of the **Cuarto Dorado**. It was probably built for Muhammad V on the occasion of his conquest of Algeciras in 1370, and was originally covered in strong colours of different tones. It reaches a peak of perfection in the impressive eaves, masterpieces of Islamic carpentry.

In a formal sense the façade served to separate the administrative and public areas from the private family quarters. The right-hand door led to domestic and service apartments, while that on the left to the heart of the palace via a right-angled passageway with no lighting but that which penetrates, dazzling, from the far end.

◄ The Façade of the Comares Palace, one of the architectural jewels of the Alhambra and of Islamic art. It was built for sultan Muhammad V in 1370 to celebrate the conquest of Algeciras by Nasrid troops

The reasoning behind the juxtaposition of the two doors is explained in an inscription carved on the arrocabe set above another frieze of mocárabes. The inscription is a poem by Ibn Zamrak, the sultan's vizier, and was composed expressly for the façade. The verses, separated by scallop shells, read thus: 'My place is that of a crown and my/ entrance a parting of the ways; the Occident believes that in me is the Orient. / Al Gani bi-llah [Muhammad V] has / charged me to let pass / the victory now being proclaimed / and I anticipate his appearance [to allow him entry], just as the horizons await to let in the dawn. / Beautify for

him, Allah, his works, as he himself is handsome of aspect and character!' (from Sp. trans. by D. CABANELAS & A. FERNÁNDEZ, 1974-1975).

Sitting on his throne between these doors and raised upon the steps, the sultan would, according to tradition, give audience and dispense justice.

◄ The proportional system of the façade allowed the development of the richest ornamentation. Although little remains of the original multi-colouring, Owen Jones left valuable information on the subject (1842-1845)

Court of the Myrtles

The patio is the most important feature in all Hispano-Islamic domestic architecture and by it the social and economic status of a family can be judged. In reality palaces are nothing but houses, on a grander scale and more highly embellished certainly, but still with the same structure and functions.

The **Court of the Myrtles** takes its name from the beds of myrtle bushes which border the pool. Originally the gardens were lower and probably filled with dwarf trees. Until the 16th century it was known as 'The Comares Court' and more recently, as 'The Court of the Pool'. This last feature plays a very important role in the architectural and aesthetic definition of the courtyard where the buildings are reflected in the mirror-like sheet of

▲ Court of the Myrtles. The courtyard is the central space in Islamic domestic architecture and around which are grouped the rooms. In palaces like that of Comares, the proportions and richness of the decoration reflect the status of the inhabitants

water, giving them greater volume and breaking the excessive horizontality of the place.

On each of the shorter sides of the courtyard are porticos which are, perhaps, the most beautiful and harmonious in all the Alhambra. Each has seven semi-circular arches, the central one being higher, and, spreading above, is the typical decoration of fretwork plaster panelling called sebka.

▲ Space and light are of prime importance here; the sheet of water that is the pool greatly contributing to the effect, as is shown by this painting of 1904 by J. M. López-Mezquita now in the Fine Arts Museum of the Alhambra.

▶ At each end of the porticos are these beautiful alcoves, spaces for respose, called alhamíes; one of them here depicted in all its decorative splendour by Owen Jones (1842-1845)

◄ The south façade of the Comares Palace, in which can be appreciated the importance of the proportional system in an architectural style that seeks perspectives from within and without

Supporting these arches are the best examples to be found of capitals carved with mocárabes. The galleries behind the porticos are covered with wooden ceilings with lazo decoration and small cupolas. At each end are alcoves with mocárabes and slightly raised above the ground; these are called alhamies.

The northern portico was originally covered by a single-slope tiled roof and with a turret on the left (as seen from the patio). It's twin, on the right, was added in the 19th century in an attempt at a symmetry that never existed.

There are two floors above the southern portico; the first has seven windows closed with wooden celosias; the upper floor is a gallery open to the courtyard through six arches and a central opening. The wooden lattice screen is late 19th century.

Palace Dwellings

On the long sides of the **Court of the Myrtles** are four sets of domestic quarters similarly arranged, with a spacious lower chamber with side alcoves and which opens to the courtyard through an

99

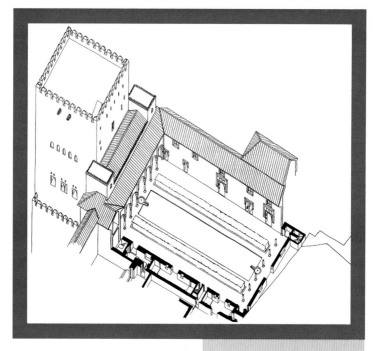

arch. All four have an upper room or algorfa with double arched windows and mullions. Access is by a staircase leading up from respective doors in the courtyard.

▲ Drawing of the Comares Palace showing details of the interiors of the dwellings which open on the sides of the Court of the Myrtles

It has been thought that these dwellings, distributed in pairs, might have been living quarters for the four wives allowed every muslim. Remodelling after the conquest effected important

▶ Photograph of the interior of the Sala de la Barca, the principal living space in the Comares Palace, taken before the fire of 1890. Its restoration was completed in 1965

changes to these buildings. The principal one being the demolition of the access to the upper floor in the southeast dwelling to make a direct connection between the **Court of the Myrtles** and the **Court of the Lions**. At the

same time an opening was made in the same building for a staircase between the **Charles V Palace** and the

Court of the Myrtles and it was also remodelled to serve as the visitor's entrance of the day.

Sala de la Barca

This is the anteroom to the most important chamber of the **Comares Palace**. The name ('Hall of the Boat') might derive from the shape of the deep ceiling, shaped like an upturned rowing-boat (Sp. barca) or perhaps from the Arabic al-baraka ('the blessing') reiterated in the stucco of the walls. At the end of the 16th century the ceiling was regilded and for this reason **101** it was also known until recently as 'The Golden Room'.

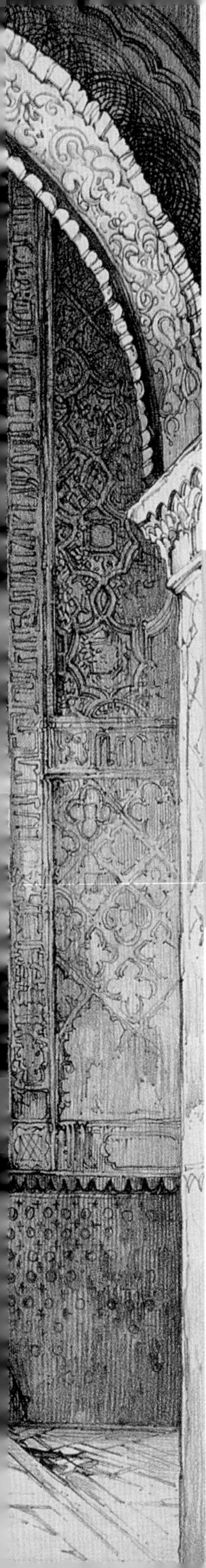

The form and dimensions of the ceiling are highly original and make it unique. The original was almost completely destroyed by fire in 1890 and restoration, based on drawings, photographs and surviving fragments, was finished in 1965. The vaulted ceiling, decorated with lazo , is of pine. The ends are semi-hemispheres with wheel decorations combining with stars and following one another about the central axis. A dado, with differing tile mosaics, runs right round the room including the alcoves behind great semi-circular arches at each end. The extremely beautiful entrance opening is very important for the lighting and visual effects it gives from the interior. It is partly closed, as if with curtains, with a false arch of mocárabes. On the soffit, or inside of the arch, are niches (Ar. taqa, Sp. tacas), one on each side, which would have contained vessels for liquids. The ornamentation is very delicate and includes, on the right and left respectively, the following verses: 'I am like the dias of a bride / endowed with beauty and perfection look at the jar and you will understand / the real truth of my words. Contemplate my diadem and see how / it appears to be a new moon's crown. But Ben Nasr is the sun in this sky / because of his dazzling splendour and beauty. May his status remain pre-eminent, / safe and secure at the time of setting sun'; 'I am the momentary prayer /

◄ Nineteenth century artists and writers discovered in the Alhambra a rich source of inspiration for the aesthetics of orientalism, as shown here by J. F. Lewis, 1835

103

whose *qibla* is an easily walked path. The jar here you may believe / to be a man standing, fulfilling his duty to pray. Notwithstanding, each time he finishes / he ought, perforce, to reiterate them. Having regard for my master Ben Nasr, / Allah ennobled his person, as being of the line of the lord of Jazray [the worthy] Sád ben Ubada' (from Sp. trans. of D. CABANELAS & A. FERNÁNDEZ, 1983-1984).

The Palace Lavatory

Alongside the Hall of the Boat, and little known due to the difficulty of visiting it, is this small room, a necessity in any home. As with other essential parts of a house, this palace lavatory, with running water, differs only in its proportion and decoration from that of any other home, humble though it be. In this case important remains have been preserved: a dado painted in tempera in earthy colours with a design reminiscent of tapestries. It probably dates from the second half of the 14th century.

Dependencies

In the spacious passage between the **Sala de la Barca** and the **Comares Hall** there is a corridor on the left which leads to the staircase to the upper rooms of the **Comares Tower** and, on the right, another leading to a small oratory. The upper rooms although traditionally interpreted as winter quarters are in fact the usual complementary spaces found in any house. As regards the oratory, neither its size nor situaton need surprise, reserved as it was for the sultan and close to the **Comares Hall**, and the alcoves of his living rooms.

◄ In Nasrid architecture the soffit of the entrance arch to the principal rooms contained a small niche, called taqa, in which were placed vessels for liquids

◄ The small oratory which allowed the sultan to recite his prayers close to both his living area and the Throne Room

105

Comares Hall

The Comares Tower, at 45 mts., is the highest in the Alhambra and contains in its interior what is also the biggest room, the Comares Hall, also called the 'Ambassadors' Hall', as well as the 'Throne Room'. Nine small alcoves open in the walls and are decorated equally in pairs, except the one in the middle opposite

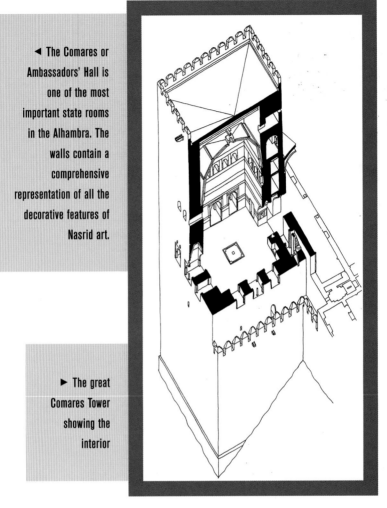

◄ The Comares or Ambassadors' Hall is one of the most important state rooms in the Alhambra. The walls contain a comprehensive representation of all the decorative features of Nasrid art.

► The great Comares Tower showing the interior

the entrance, which was reserved for the sultan and is more richly decorated. The flooring, re-made on several occasions, preserves in the centre most of the original pieces of gilt lustre ware and other similar pieces were added later. There might also have been marble floor-slabs. The walls are entirely covered with decoration. The lower part preserves the original dados of varying mosaic tiling above which stretch stucco panels in which geometric (with ataurique, vegetal **107** decoration) and epigraphic motifs alternate.

Originally they were highly coloured as if they were tapestries. Apart from its ornamental value, the epigraphy is no less important as an expression of politico-religious purpose. Here are three examples of maxims repeated all over the hall:

'Eternity is an attribute of Allah';
'Delight in good, for surely it is Allah who assists';
'To Allah alone belongs grandeur, glory, eternity, empire and power'.

Although it is difficult to highlight any one feature amongst so many in this hall, the wooden ceiling possibly stands out for the originality of its conception and execution. The ceiling is made up of a series of different sized boards nailed together and then to the ribs of the vault,

◄ Detail of the decoration in the Comares Hall, by Owen Jones (1842- 1845)

which is itself supported from the walls by beams; the varying small decorative wooden pieces were then pinned to the boards. In this way is formed, by the superimposition of planes, a three dimensional effect and a geometric layout full of significance: a pyramidal stepping sequence in which figure the seven heavens of the cosmos through which, according to

▲ The ceiling of the Comares Hall is a masterpiece of Hispano-Islamic carpentry; shown here as it would have been with the original colouring

▶ Diagram of the eight heavens in the ceiling of the Comares Hall

110 Islamic eschatology, the soul travels until reaching, at the peak, the eighth (represented in the ceiling by the

small cupola of mocárabes) wherein resides Allah and whence radiates His power. The heavens are represented by successive bands of stars, set in different planes, made up of geometric pieces, multicoloured in varying tones. Along the four sides of the ceiling, emphazising its symbolism, and starting on the north side, runs *Sura 67* from the Qur'an, entitled *al-Mulk* ('Sovereignty'): 'Blessed be He in whose hands is the sovereignty and He has power over everything. He who created death and life so as to test you as to whoever of you is fairer in action. He is the All-Mighty, the All-forgiving. He who has created seven stratified heavens. You do not see any discrepancy in the creation of the Compassionate. So fix your gaze, do you see any flaws? Then, fix your gaze again and again, and your gaze will recoil back to you discomforted and weary. We have adorned the lower heaven with lamps, and We turned them into missiles launched against the devils; and We have prepared for them the punishment of the fire' (trans. by MAJID FAKHRY, 1997).

Entrance to the Bath

The original entry to the **Comares Bath** was by the little door on the left, nearest the royal rooms of the palace. Inside it was then more complex than now,

► After the conquest of Granada the Catholic Monarchs reserved the palaces of Comares and the Lions for their personal use, connecting them with the straight corridor shown here on the right of the photograph

with a right-angle bend and rooms for the bath attendant. The present entrance gives directly on to the apoditerium (Ar. Bayt al-maslaj). This first room in the bath served as a changing room. It has an alcove set behind a double arch and is on the same level as the **Court of the Myrtles**. Opposite the alcove a staircase descends to the **Sala de las Camas** or relaxing room; the second apoditerium in the bath. Although this last can be viewed from the outside (in the **Patio de Lindaraja**) visits to the bath, given its special nature, are restricted to certain times.

Connection between Palaces

The difference in concept and use of domestic space between Muslims and Christians meant that the latter would often aquire two Islamic houses instead of one and open a

▲ The Court of the Lions according to P. J. Girault de Prangey (1837)

connection between them, so-by adapting the building to their particular needs. This happened in the Alhambra; the Catholic Monarchs, for example, making a direct connection between the **Comares Palace** and the **Palace of the Lions**. These palaces had formerly been independent, although they were complementary within the structure of the royal court and their nuclei on the same level. And so it is that today, as has been mentioned, the connection between the two is a straight passageway through rooms in the **Court of the Myrtles** which leads **113** to the **Sala de los Mocárabes** and then the **Court of the Lions**.

The Palace of the Lions

Muhammad V was the inspirer of this beautiful palace, constructed between 1362 and 1391, in the second part of his divided rule. With him the Nasrid sultanate reached its apogee and in many ways the **Palace of the Lions** represents a synthesis of all the stages of its artistic development. Recent research has described it as 'The Palace of the Riyad' or 'of the Garden', since there was one here before the present buildings. It is at right-angles to the axis of the **Comares Palace** and differences between the two are considerable, above all in the type of patio, which is here cruciform and with a central fountain. Precedents for the patio as well as its subsequent influence, are found as much in Islamic Spain as in the rest of the Islamic world. It is a symbolic representation of Paradise which, according to the Christian and Islamic religions, is divided symmetrically into four parts separated by rivers or channels which meet at the central fountain. It is not known for certain whether the four parts were paved or if there were gardens.

▲ All the decoration in the palaces was originally multicoloured and from the 19th century onwards, many artists reproduced it in plates such as this one, details from the Palace of the Lions, by P. J. Girault de Prangey (1837)

The Pavilions

The importance of the cruciform, which indicates the four cardinal points, is underlined by the two pavilions —like chapels or oriental kiosks covered by their corresponding cupolas— which project along the main east-west axis centred on the water-washed basin of the fountain. The play of the semi-circular and stilted arches with

'curtains' of mocárabes, together with the positioning of the columns, make these pavilions one of the most delicate expressions of the Nasrid interior as well as suggestive of the sensuality and delight of nature. They are a veritable highpoint in romantic orientalism in the west. The unbroken sequence of arches and columns with its complex rhythms, and the plaster celosias around the court, reinforce this magical image so universally admired.

▲ The famous Fountain of the Lions was originally richly coloured with a predominance of gilding, which would have stood out against the white background of the marble, especially the beautiful poem inscribed around the edge of the basin

The Fountain

This gives the palace its name and was possibly inspired by the fountain, called 'The Sea of Bronze', described in the Bible as being at the entrance to Solomon's

Temple in Jerusalem and which was supported by the bulls of the twelve tribes of Israel. Tradition has it that there was a similar fountain in the disappeared palace of Yusuf ben Nagrella, a Jewish vizier of the 11th century, which was located in the present **Alcazaba**.

The **Fountain of the Lions** was carved, in marble, expressly for the Nasrid palace. Originally it would have been richly painted, with a predominance of gold, which would stand out from the white marble background. Around the rim is a poem by Ibn Zamrak, which, with lovely

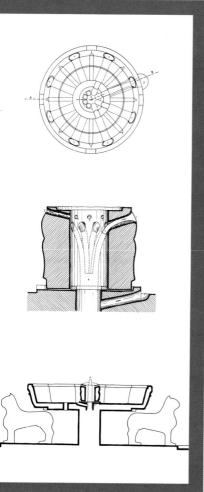

◄ Plan and section of the original cylinder in the middle of the basin which served to regulate the flow of water in the Fountain of the Lions. It is now in the Alhambra Museum

metaphors, praises and explains the complicated, but perfect, hydraulic system which fills and empties the fountain: 'Blessed be He who gave to the Imam Muhammad, noble ideas with which to grace his mansions. / For are there not marvels in this garden / which Allah has made incomparable in beauty / and a sculpture of pearls of transparent clarity whose **117** edges are trimmed with dewdrops? / Melted silver runs between the pearls, / one as the other in beauty, white and pure. / Water and marble seem as one, / so we know not which of the two flows. / Do you not see how the water spills over the basin, / but is hidden forthwith in the channels? / It is a lover whose eyelids brim with tears; tears which then hide in fear of betrayal. / Is it not, in reality, but a white mist emptying its waters on the lions / and resembling the hand of the caliph, which, in the morning, lavishes favours on the lions of war? / He who beholds the lions in menacing attitude, [knows that] only respect [for the Emir] contains their fury. / Oh, descendent of the Companions [of the Prophet Muhammad], and by no indirect lineage, a heritage of nobility, which even the conceited esteem, / may the peace of Allah be with you and keep you safe, repeating over your celebrations and casting down your enemies!' (from Sp. trans. by D. CABANELAS & A. FERNÁNDEZ, 1979-1981).

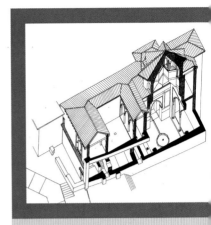

▲ Detail of the internal structure of the Sala de los Abencerrajes. On the second floor (left) is the so-called Patio of the Harem and, underneath it, the cistern for the Comares bath

Sala de los Mocárabes

The **Palace of the Lions** is structured around two living areas and two others whose purpose is ambivalent. The first of these last two is the **Sala de los Mocárabes**, which, being next to the principal entrance to the palace, must have served as a vestibule or reception room. Access to

this entrance is through three great arches with mocárabes, which served for illumination and ventilation and
which at the same time offer from the inside, a perspec-
tive of the patio. The name of the room derives from a
vaulted ceiling of mocárabes which originally covered it
but which was irreparably damaged when a near-by gunpowder store exploded in 1590. The remains were then
demolished and partially substituted, in the first deca-
des of the 17th century, by a late renaissance ceiling by
the painter and architect, Blas de Ledesma.

Sala de los Abencerrajes

This is the southern residential area. Its name,
which dates from the 16th century, records a dubious

◄ Interior of the Sala de los
Abencerrajes, lying on one of the
axes of the Court which cross at
the Fountain of the Lions

tradition that it was the
scene of bloody con-
frontations between
court factions that left
dead leading members
of the Abencerrajes, a
north African tribe.
The principal room is
raised above the level
of the patio which is
viewed from the inte-
rior through the only

119

opening, the great door, which retains its original leaves and jambs. In the centre is a marble fountain. On either side are spacious alcoves separated from the room by pairs of arches. A great part of the stucco decoration was modified in the 16th century,

▲ The cupolas of mocárabes in this palace reflect the maximum splendour of Nasrid architectural decoration. This one, of the Abencerrajes, forms a beautiful eight-pointed star which seems to rotate on the square room below

which is also the date of the dado of Sevillian tiles.

120   But the most spectacular feature of the room is the cupola of mocárabes forming an eight-pointed star, which, like an image of the universe seems to girate on the eight squinches which link the terrestrial lower floor, square in plan, with heaven above, poligonal.

Behind the door are two much remodelled passages which lead respectively, to a now diappeared lavatory and to the upper floor where there is a room or algorfa. It has a complementary patio, modest and secluded, called the **Patio del Harem**, which still preserves dados with mural paintings and two black marble capitals (12th -13th century) re-used here. Access is restricted.

Sala de los Reyes

This is the great emblematic area of the court and palace; a place for receptions and relaxing in. It is structured around a great hall 30 mts. long which served as the setting for the greatest variety of celebrations. Along the back and at the extremes are five alcoves opened by wide arches with mocárabes forming 'curtains'.

▼ The Sala de los Reyes was the emblematic leisure and ceremonial area of the court, with the spaces along its length masterfully separated by arches of mocárabes and aired and lit from the patio

The hall consists of three square-plan units in front of each alcove and open to the portico and covered with cupolas which extend above the roof as lantern ceilings —another characteristic of Nasrid architecture— The units are separated along the length of the hall by great

121

double arches with mocárabes at right-angles to the long sides, creating that particular play of light which makes this hall another of the most attractive places

▲ A colourful Court of the Lions as pictured by E. Gerhardt in 1860

in the Alhambra. Its name ('Hall of the Kings') comes from the representation of the ten people in the ceiling of the central alcove which, together with paintings on the ceilings of the alcoves on either side, is one of the artistic curiosities of the palace. The three ceilings are wooden vaults in the shape of an upturned boat, made up of different sized boards assembled with tacks. The paintings are realized on sheep-

skin fixed to the wood with paste and small bamboo pins. Over these skins was spread a water-based fish-bone glue and several layers of plaster on which the profiles of the figures were traced out, then painted in with colours mixed with egg yolk and varnished. For a time it was thought that these personages were the sultans of the Nasrid dynasty or perhaps judges meeting in a High Court, and from this last comes the name 'Sala de la Justicia' ('Hall of Justice'), but nowadays it is difficult to be sure. The other two

▲ The alcoves in the Sala de los Reyes are covered with masterly painted vaults, probably by Genoese artists, in tempera on sheep skin. The central one represents an animated assembly of notables

▼ The painted vaults in the side alcoves represent courtly scences of great iconographic value. Isidoro Marín painted this watercolour, now in the Alhambra Museum, of a hunting scene from one of them (1921)

paintings represent romances or courtly tales in a medieval setting, in which Christian and Muslim knights meet up, fight with savage beasts or play a game of chess; with a lady, a castle and a garden always present. These are themes, and above all representational forms, somewhat alien to Islamic tradition with its dislike of detailed pictorial scenes. In fact the style is clearly western, suggesting artists of the Avignon or north Italian circles of the 14th century. It should be remembered that there was a thriving colony of Genoese silk merchants in Nasrid Granada who would have had contacts with Christian artists. These would not, of course, have had the Muslim's reluctance to depict such scenes.

Sala de Dos Hermanas

This hall is opposite the **Sala de Abencerrajes**; both have a similar structure and identical purpose. The original door here is also very decorative and it has been removed to be exhibited in the **Alhambra Museum**.

According to tradition the name ('Hall of Two Sisters'), comes from the two great marble slabs either side of the small fountain, but a recent interpretation of the poem quoted below suggests that this duality refers to a line from the Qur'an. The dado of alicatados is a geometrical composition **124** based on interlacing ribbons of different colours and one of the most original in the Alhambra. Stucco decoration, divid-

ed in great panels separated by epigraphic texts, covers the walls, culminating in the masterpiece of the hall: the cupola of mocárabes. Starting from a central star the stalactites multiply to include a total, by Owen Jones's count, of five thousand of these tiny hanging prisms.

On either side are alcoves, each with the usual space for a tarima or bed, and covered with extraordinary artesonados, **125** the decorative wooden ceilings.

▲ The Sala de Dos Hermanas is covered by an impressive vault, as a poem inscribed on the walls says: 'Sublime piece of work ! Fortune wishes it to surpass all other monuments..'

► On the surface of the walls, above the original tiling of interlacing bands, is one of the most beautiful poems in the Alhambra, composed on the occasion of the circumcision of the sultan's son

▲ Owen Jones 'dismantled' the parts
of the cupola of the Sala de Dos
Hermanas and drew this plan and
section (1842-45)

On the occasion of the circumcision (one of the most important celebrations in the Islamic world) of his son, Muhammad V, Abu Abd Allah, commissioned his vizier and court poet, Ibn Zamrak, to compose the poem inscribed on the wall of this hall. It is one of the longest inscriptions in the Alhambra with twenty-four verses, within cartouches and medallions, distributed starting from the angle on the right as one enters, with three verses in each side between angles: 'A garden am I, by beauty adorned: you will know me what I am if you look at my delights. / For Muhammad, my sultan, elevates me to the most noble that ever will be or has been. / Sublime piece of work, Fortune wishes me to surpass all other monuments! / What

diversion is here for the eye! Here the noble [person] renews his appetite for beauty. / The Pleides serve him as an amulet; the breeze protects him with its magic. Without peer, a brilliant cupola shines, of beautiful highlights and hidden corners. / Overcome, Gemini streches out a hand; the moon comes along to converse. The stars wish to be encrusted here and revolve no more in the celestial wheel, / and in both patios submissively and faithfully serve him as slaves. / It is no wonder that they err and tresspass their assigned limits, ready to serve my lord, who serves the Glorious [One] and thereby himself achieves Glory. / The

▲ The Sala de los Ajimeces owes its name to the overhanging balconies closed by celosias which would have existed in the windows. This engraving of it is after A. Laborde (1837)

portico is so beautiful, that the palace with the celestial vault competes. / With such lovely gossamer you dressed it, that you leave the looms of Yemen forgotten. / How many arches climb to its summit, on columns adorned by the light, / like celestials spheres which revolve about the shining pillar of the dawn ! / The columns are so lovely in every way, that chattering tongues spread their fame: / the marble throws off its clear light, which invades the corner darkened by shadow; / its reflections become iridescent and you would say, despite of their size, that they are pearls. / We never saw such sublimity reached, or surroundings more light and spacious. / We never saw a garden more blooming, never knew a harvest sweeter, nor sensed such fragrance. / By permission of the judge of Beauty it pays, twice over, its taxes with two coins, / since, at dawn, Zephir comes with silver drachmas enough to pay in its hands, / and then throws between the branches of the trees, golden dirhams of the sun, to adorn the wood. / Kinship links it to victory: only to him of the sultan is ceded this privilege' (from Sp. trans, by E. GARCÍA GÓMEZ, 1975).

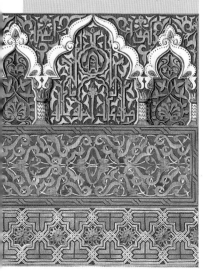

▼ The decoration in the Lindaraja area is among the most spectacular in the Alhambra. This detail of the soffit of the entrance arch to the Sala de Dos Hermanas is by P. J. Girault de Prangey (1837)

Sala de los Ajimeces

The hall receives its name from the ajimeces which would originally have closed off the twin windows on either side of the wall. Ajimeces were overhanging wooden balconies with celosias, **129** much used in Nasrid archi-

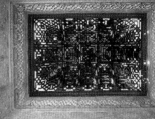

tecture, but of which hardly any survive, although the idea has been used in convents of the enclosed orders and in the popular architecture of Andalusia.

Entry to the hall is through a great arch with dog-tooth moulding and the typical niches in the soffits. The mural decoration of the upper part is of multi-coloured stucco, but the lower part is left undecorated, perhaps to hang tapestries. The vault with mocárabes was re-made in the first third of the 16th century.

Mirador de Lindaraja

Completing the symmetrical axis of the **Sala de Dos Hermanas**, is this small square space, whose raison d'être as a look-out (Sp. mirador, atalaya) was the view out over the

Albayzín and the countryside. The name, 'Eyes of Aixa's house' (Ar. *ayn dar Aisa*, Sp. corrp. 'Lindaraja') indicates this, as does the testimony of almost all visitors, starting with Charles V, who liked to have supper here. Stretching down below it originally, was a garden.

The interior surfaces of the mirador are a perfect summing-up of the concept of proportion in Nasrid decorative architectural design. It has led some writers to consider it the clearest example of a supposed 'Nasrid baroque'. Spreading down under a blind arch of mocárabes is the multi-coloured stucco, basically epigraphic, which frames a mullioned or double-arch window with central column. This window, like those on either side, opens low down so as to allow a view of the landscape while seated on the floor with an elbow on the parapet. The mosaic tiling in the soffits of the arch is made of smaller pieces than usual and has a very beautiful metallic sheen.

A false ceiling with stained glass pieces, a real archaeological jewel, closes of the upper part of this room, for some perhaps the most notable of all in the **Palace of the Lions** and naturally, that most appreciated by the Romantics and lovers of Islamic culture.

◄ In the soffit of the entrance arch to the Mirador de Lindaraja are panels of mosaic tiling which, for the reduced size of the pieces and exquisite workmanship, are probably the most beautiful in all the Alhambra

131

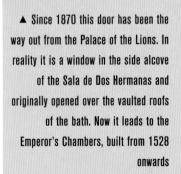

▲ Since 1870 this door has been the way out from the Palace of the Lions. In reality it is a window in the side alcove of the Sala de Dos Hermanas and originally opened over the vaulted roofs of the bath. Now it leads to the Emperor's Chambers, built from 1528 onwards

► Plan of the Lindaraja area with itinerary marked

The Lindaraja area

The exit from the Sala de Dos Hermanas

The connection between various parts of the Alhambra has been modified over the ages. Thus, for example, the original entrances to the **Palace of the Lions** were on its southern side, while the exit, from 1870 onwards, and now within the visitors itinerary, was made from the western alcove of the **Sala de Dos Hermanas**. The small opening which forms the exit, was originally a window of the same size and proportions as that in the alcove opposite. The window gave a view out over the vaults of the **Bath**, today to be seen from the corridor made in the 16th century to link up with the **Emperor's Chambers**.

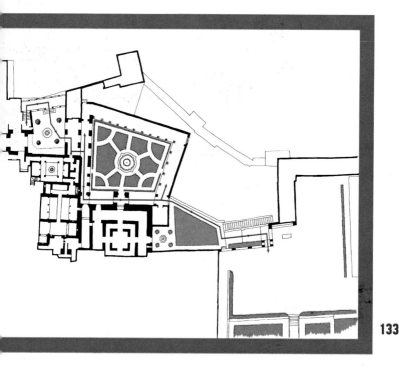

The Emperor's Chambers

▲ The Emperor's study is among the buildings added to the Nasrid palaces in the 16th century. Of note is the coffered ceiling designed by Pedro Machuca around 1532

At the end of the corridor is the first of the six 'new quarters', which Charles V had built in 1528 while his palace was being constructed. It can be identified as 'the study', and has a chimneypiece and a coffered ceiling, designed in 1532 by Pedro Machuca. Further along is an antechamber to the royal bedrooms. Above the door is a stone plaque, put up in 1914 by the first Patronato de la Alhambra, in memory of Washington Irving, American author of *Tales of the Alhambra*, who stayed in adjacent rooms in 1829. These are known as 'The Fruit Rooms' after the

▲ The building of the Emperor's Chambers formed this small Patio de la Reja, named after the running balcony and grille, made in 1654, which dominates it

ceilings which were painted with this motif in about 1537 by Julio Aquiles and Alejandro Mayner, disciples of Raphael.

▲ The Patio de Lindaraja acquired its present cloistered aspect in the 16th century. Originally it was a lower garden of the Palace of the Lions and open to the landscape

The special nature of these rooms means that they are not included in the official itinerary, but they may be visited by previous arrangement at certain times.

The Gallery, Patio de la Reja and Peinador de la Reina

The antechamber of the **Emperor's Chambers** gives on to an open gallery with delightful views of the Albaycin and the Sacromonte. This corridor, built by Christian kings in the 16th century, used to have renaissance alfresco paintings, but these have disappeared. It leads to the so-called **Peinador de la Reina** or 'Queen's Dressing Room' a small floor added to the tower of the same name. The interior, rectangular in plan, heated from below and designed in Italianate style, contains important murals painted between 1537 and 1539, also by Arquiles and Mayner. They represent the expedition sent by Charles V to conquer Tunis, as well as including grotesques and mythological motifs and extend to the adjoining gallery which surrounds what must have been the antique lantern part of the tower open on three sides with elliptical arches, making a singular 'atalaya' or look-out. It is open to limited guided tours only.

Between the **Emperor's Chambers** and the **Comares Tower** is the **Patio de la Reja**, so called after the wrought iron grille (Sp. reja) of the running balcony, made between 1654 and 1655 to protect the rooms behind. Two galleries one above the other, close off this space on the northern side; the upper gallery connects the **Comares Tower** with the Christian buildings and was formed in 1618 making use of columns and capitals brought from different parts of the Alhambra. Some of them, considered mast-

▶ The Sala de las Camas in the Comares Palace bath, with the atmosphere given it by M. Vico in 1887

erpieces, have been removed and are now exhibited in the **Alhambra Museum**. The lower gallery makes a pretty arbour.

In the west side is an opening from which may be seen the basement of the **Sala de la Barca** and known from the 17th century as 'Room of the Nymphs' after some classical statues once stored there.

Baño de Comares

From the gallery which separates the **Patio de la Reja** and the **Patio de Lindaraja**, there is an entry to the lower floor of the **Comares Bath** (the original entrance, it will be remembered, is at the higher level of the **Court of**

the **Myrtles**). This lower entry leads to the **Sala de las Camas** ('of the beds'), equivalent to the *apoditerium* in Roman baths. It was a place to relax in and for private grooming attentions before the bath and is lit by a lantern roof around which, on the upper floor, are distributed the rooms of the bath attendant. The loud colours of the room are not orig-

inal, but those painted in a restoration in the second half of the 19th century. The vaulted ceilings of the steam rooms, following on,

◄ Interior of the Comares Bath, the vaulted ceilings are covered with skylights to light and air the rooms

▲ A special shoe to give protection from the hot floor of the bath. It was found in the Alhambra and is now in the Alhambra Museum

▼ Drawing showing the situation of the Comares Bath in relation to the Court of the Myrtles and other palace dependencies

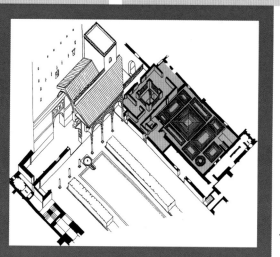

have the characteristic star-shaped skylights which, with
140 glass coverings opening from above, regulate the density
of steam in the rooms and air them. Beneath the marble

floor and between the walls, different pipes warmed the rooms with steam and hot air from the boilers in the furnaces where the water was heated.

The biggest room, with a double arcade and the following, with two great marble pillars, were the hottest in the baths and footwear would have been worn as protection. The ceramic dados were installed in the 16th century to adapt the baths to western taste.

Patio de Lindaraja

This opens from the **Patio de la Reja** and is similar in structure but more cloister-like. The name comes from the mirador in the **Palace of the Lions** and, as has been said, before it was closed off by the **Emperor's Chambers**, enjoyed an open prospect of the Albayzin. In fact, the original Islamic garden was left enclosed by the three bays of rooms

◄ One of the places in the Alhambra that has most attracted artists over the years is the Patio de Lindaraja, probably because of its light and atmosphere, captured here in a painting of 1910 by Joaquin Sorolla

above colonnades on the ground floor. The columns were brought here from elsewhere and give the patio a cloistered air, accentuated by the style of the garden and the central fountain. This is a baroque design by Bartolomé Fernández Lechuga, which incorporated a magnificent Nasrid basin that is in the **Alhambra Museum**; the one here now being a copy. The way out from the **Patio de Lindaraja** and from the route through the palaces, is through the eastern bay, the upper floor of which was called, until recently, 'The Chateaubriand Gallery', after the celebrated French writer and politician who left his signature inscribed there. **141**

El Partal

This is the name given to the area which extends in front of the exit from the **Patio de Lindaraja** and made up of gardens and esplanades grouped around what is left of an old palace. The gardens were designed in the first third of the 20th century and incorporate archaeological and architectural remains.

The original layout of the area was a series of terraces which, following the rise of the land, ascend from the walls of the fortress over the left bank of the Darro to the upper ward of the Alhambra. It is probable that it was here that the first palaces planned by the Nasrids were built.

▲ The Palacio del Pórtico is named after the portico or gallery, so characteristic of Nasrid architecture, built on the short side of the patio in front of the principal room

El Palacio del Pórtico

Of the few remains left in the Partal those of the **Palacio del Pórtico** are the most important, presiding over the whole area from the edge of the wall and having a similar layout to the **Comares Palace**. That is to say; a great rectangular pool crowned by the gallery of the portico, in this case of just five arches, and behind which is the principal room inside the **Torre de las Damas** ('of the **142** ladies'). The surface decoration consists of the usual dado of coloured tiling, wide panels of stucco originally multi-

coloured and with an exceptionally richly decorated wooden ceiling. This is now in the Museum für Islamische Kunst in Berlin, since up until 1891 these rooms were the private property of a German, Arthur von Gwinner.

▼ General plan of the palace and its gardens

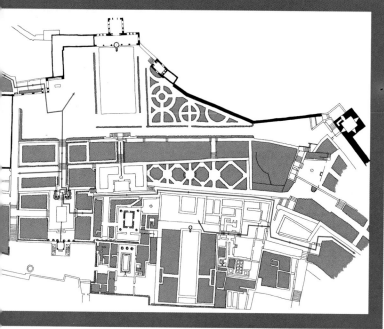

From the decorative style of the whole, its construction has been attributed to the time of Muhammad III (1302-1309), which makes it the oldest of all surviving **143** palaces in the Alhambra.

Alongside the **Torre de las Damas**, above the portico, rises a small and beautiful mirador very characteristic of Nasrid architecture and which, for its exception views, is now called

▲ This is the original ceiling of the Torre de las Damas, now in the Museum of Islamic Art in Berlin

'The Observatory'. The special nature of this building means that it cannot be visited.

Oratory and nearby houses

Alongside the portico of the palace is a tiny building, rectangular in plan, whose decoration dates it to the time of Yusuf I. It is an oratory, with its *mihrab* **144** properly orientated and which, as is traditional in the Alhambra, blends into the landscape. On the opposite side, the portico is extended by a row of small morisco houses, also built on top of the walls, and in whose interior are preserved fragments of the exterior painting of the portico, as well as a mural painting with Nasrid courtly scenes. Visits are restricted due to its importance and fragile state.

Climbing up in front of the **Partal** area is a succession of gardened terraces. In the first, making a perfect axis with the portico, are the remains of a small pavilion which belonged to this palace and which closed off its southern side.

▼ Alongside the portico of the Partal is an Oratory within an independent building of later date. Like all Islamic religious buildings, it is orientated towards Mecca

Back towards the exterior walls of the **Palace of the Lions** is a staircase from which, on the right, may be visited what has erroneously been called the Rauda. It is an impressive tower, square in plan, with a magnificent cupola with mocárabe squinches. It is a *qubba* or pavilion open on three sides with great horseshoe arches, the fourth side serves as a communicating door to the interior of the **Palace of the Lions**, proving its role as a connection between these two palaces. The walk through the

145

▲ Between the hanging terraces of the Partal was a network of streets connecting the several parts of the building; today they form attractive garden walks. On the right in the photograph is the end wall of the Palacio de Yusuf III, which later passed to the conde de Tendilla, governor of the Alhambra after the Christian conquest

◄ The building known as Puerta de la Rauda for its proximity to the cemetery (rauda) of the sultans of the Alhambra. It is one of the oldest parts of the palaces, originally free-standing it served as a connection between them. Inside is a magnificent cupola with mocárabe squinches

gardens continues under an ivy pergola leading to the **Patio de los Nenúfares** ('water lilies') with a central pond and which today serves as a distribution point for the visit. To the left (east) the official route leads to the Generalife by way of the **Towers Walk**, while the other option, on the right (west) is the way out from the palaces and leads to the **Calle Real**; this option allows a visit to the **Alcazaba** or to the **Charles V Palace** for those who have not already done so, as well as the exit from the monument to descend to Granada or, following upwards the **Calle Real**, an alternative route to the Generalife or the car park. This second option leads passed what is left of the true Rauda, or cemetery, of the Nasrid sultans from Muhammad III (1302-1309) onwards and whose remains were exhumed at the end of the 15th century by Boabdil, the last Nasrid sultan, to be reburied elsewhere. Some of the richly inscribed tombstones and decoration from the cemetery are preserved in the **Alhambra Museum**.

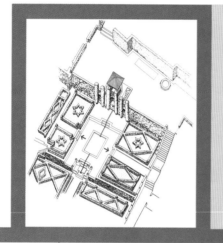

◄ Patio de los Nenúfares (water-lilies) in the Partal Gardens. From here the Towers Walk (left; east) leads to the Generalife and in the opposite direction (right; west) to the way out to the Calle Real, the Charles V Palace and the Alcazaba

▼ Plan of the Rauda or cemetary of the sultans

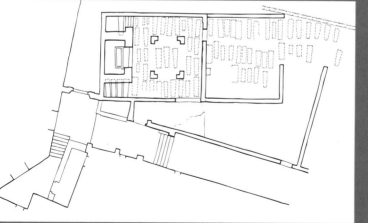

The Towers Walk

The start of this walk is an ideal spot to view the portico of the Partal to the north. This cobbled path was perhaps the lower 'Calle Real' whose function was to connect the different palaces of the area. One of these, the **Palacio de Yusuf III** (1408-1417), identifiable only by its archaeological remains, is on the right. It is of the same type as the **Palacio del Pórtico** and the **Comares Palace** and was granted by the Catholic Monarchs to the conde de Tendilla as the official residence of the alcaides or governors of the Alhmabra. The walk continues, with views of the Generalife, passed the Towers spaced out along this north-east section of the wall.

► The platform of the Palacio de Yusuf III with the base of the principal tower at the back. Before it would have been the traditional portico in front of the pool. In the foreground are the remains of the palace bath

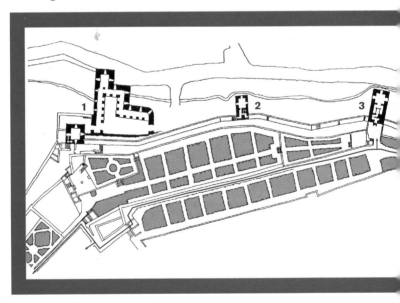

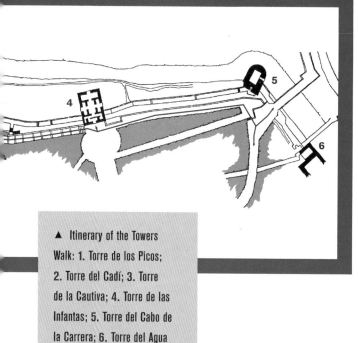

▲ Itinerary of the Towers Walk: 1. Torre de los Picos; 2. Torre del Cadí; 3. Torre de la Cautiva; 4. Torre de las Infantas; 5. Torre del Cabo de la Carrera; 6. Torre del Agua

The first of these is the **Torre de los Picos** ('spikes'), so called after the projecting corbels, remains of machiolation, which now look rather like bird beaks, on the corners and meant to protect the **Puerta del Arrabal** ('of the outskirts') at its foot. This is one of the four exterior gates of the Alhambra and may be visted at special times. The **Torre**

◀ Towers Walk. So called for the course it takes along the main walls of the precinct on which alternate towers of different sizes and purposes. There are fine views over to the Generalife and its gardens

del Cadí ('judge') is next, guarding this section of the wall and from whose foot ascends, between orchards and vegetable gardens

▶ Interior of the principal room in the Torre de la Cautiva, probably one of the most notable in the Alhambra for both its structure and decoration

and protected by stout walls, the lower entrance way to the Generalife.

Torre de la Cautiva

The exterior of this tower ('of the lady prisoner') is little different from the others; only the proportions and a few constructional details distinguish, from the outside, the different towers along this wall.

However, the decoration of the interior spaces of this one is among the most outstanding in the Alhambra. It is in fact a tower-palace whose structure and layout is the same as that of other houses and palaces of the monument, with a right-angle bend to the entrance and a patio beyond with arches on pillars. The principal room is square in plan with double windows forming small alcoves. This room, together with the **Comares Hall**, possesses the most complete decorative scheme in the Alhambra and it is no surprise that it dates, like that hall, from the time of Yusuf I (1333-1354). A poem inscribed starting on the left of the room gives the key to understanding it: 'This room is here to adorn the Alhambra; it is home to both the peaceable and to warriors; / a Qalahurra . Say, is it not at once a fortress and a mansion of joy! / It is a palace in which splendour is shared out among its ceiling, its floor and its four walls; / there are marvels in the stucco and in the tiling, but / the worked wooden pieces of its ceiling are more extraordinary still; / there were joined and their union formed the most perfect of constructions, where already existed the noblest of mansions' (from the Sp. trans by Mª. JESÚS RUBIERA, 1994).

152   Only a limited number of people may visit the tower and then at special times.

Ronda or Foso

Entrance to the **Torre de la Cautiva** is from the level ground of the Medina and crossing a foso (fosse or trench) by a sort of bridge. For this reason it is one of the best places for understanding the working of the defensive structure of the fortress. The exterior wall enclosing the palatine city has a walk-way along the top with a parapet on the outer edge —some streches still have the battlements— called the adarve, which served the watch or guard making its round. Where the walk-way met some of the towers, for example here and in the next tower along, the **Torre de las Infantas**, it passed underneath through a tunnel so as to remain independent and not interfere in the domestic life above.

As well as this walk-way on top of the walls, on the inside face of the wall, running alonside and following its whole length —1,150 mts.— is a wide sunken trench called **Foso** (fosse) or **Calle de Ronda** (passage of the rounds), since it served both purposes; to connect various parts of the the city and act as a defensive belt in times of seige. As with the adarve, so as not to break the access to some of the towers, it passes under a wide bridge making it in some places a real tunnel.

▲ The inside face of the Alhambra wall has a sunken walkway along its whole length which by means of tunnels and galleries passes towers like that of the Infantas

153

Torre de las Infantas

Leaving the previous tower behind, the **Towers Walk** now changes direction and follows more closely the wall, and climbing with the contours, reveals the **Torre de las Infantas** ('of the princesses'). In the entrance, of three right-angle bends, **154** the small vault with large painted mocárabes is of note. The principal rooms are distributed about a central court with a small polygonal fountain. It would originally have been covered with a cupola lantern ceiling with mocárabes, but now has a modern wooden one. Athough the decoration is similar to that in the **Torre de la Cautiva**, it is in fact later, dating from the reign of Muhammad VII (1392-1408).

The tower is the scene of a famous legend, retold by Washington Irving, of the three princesses Zaida, Zorayda and Zorahaida.

The Upper Alhambra

◄ The inside of the Torre de las Infantas as seen by P. J. Girault de Prangey in 1837

▲ Doorway and bridge of the Upper Alhambra at the eastern extreme of the fortress. It is the present and most direct connection between the Alhambra and the Generalife

After the last stretch alongside the walls, the **Towers Walk** finishes beside the **Torre del Cabo de la Carrera**. According to an inscription now disappeared, it was constructed for the Catholic Monarchs in 1502. The tower, like all those in this part of the Alhambra, including the Torre del Agua ('water') a little further along, was partly blown-up by the French in the Napoleonic Wars. This area, much altered, today serves to link different tourist itineraries. Thus, on the left is a great portal opening in the wall, which, over a bridge, connects directly and easily with the Generalife as well as the way out and car park. To the right is the Calle Real leading back to the interior of the Alhambra, the Alcazaba, the **155** Charles V Palace and the Nasrid Palaces.

El Generalife

The Almunia of the Generalife

The almunia or royal home farm was planned as an agricultural estate and a place to relax in, with a nucleus of residential buildings and a huge extension of cultivated and grazing land divided into four large

◄ View of the Generalife with the palace in the background above the surrounding gardens and orchards. The New Gardens and the amphitheatre were added in the middle of this century

▼ Aerial view of the gardens and fields of the Generalife with the Alhambra walls and, below, part of the New Gardens

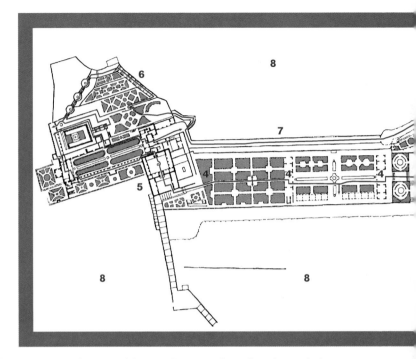

plots of vegetable gardens and orchards with hanging terraces and delimited by thick retaining walls, some of which may still be seen. Each plot has a name passed down from over the centuries and their present boundaries probably coincide, more or less, with those of medieval times. Ringing the estate were meadows used for breeding horses, for farm animals or even as a hunting chase for the sultan.

The name Generalife has been variously interpreted over its history, from 'Garden' or 'Garden of the Zambra dancer', 'The highest of gardens' or 'house of craftsmanship' to 'Mansion of pleasure or great recreation' and 'Garden of the zither player'. Today the commonly accepted meaning is **Garden** or **Jardines del Alarife**, that is 'Gardens of the builder or architect'.

After the conquest in 1492 the Catholic Monarchs **158** granted custody and use of the estate to an alcaide (military governor). It passed, in 1631, to the Granada-Venegas

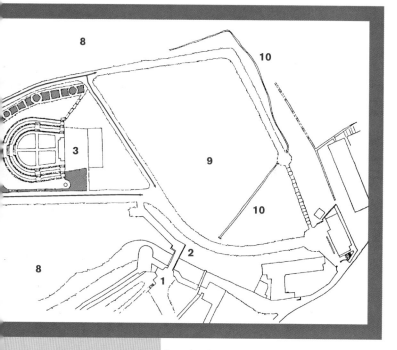

family, but now in perpetuity, until, after a long legal battle started in the last century, it was ceded to the state in 1921.

Originally there were several entrances and evidence remains of at least three of them. The most direct connected the **Almunia del Generalife** with the Alhambra through the fields. Another was through the main gate where the farm and garden workers lived and still to be seen alongside the **Entrance Pavilion**. The third was through the **Postigo de los Carneros** ('sheep wicket') in the highest part of the estate. Today however, the official itinerary starts between an avenue of cypresses, planted to commemorate the visit of Isabel II in **159**

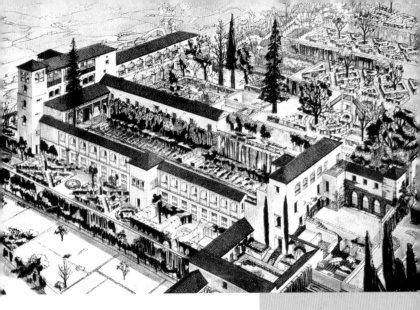

1862. This is one of three official itineraries through the whole Alhambra complex and, as has been indicated, may be taken before or after the Alhambra proper.

The New Gardens

After the definitive incorporation of the Generalife with the Alhambra it was decided to create a public park here and the result was the planting of gardens between the Alhambra and the buildings of the **Palacio del Generalife**. In fact, it was divided into three parts, created successively, which now form the **New Gardens**. The first, closest to the palace, was started in 1931 as a garden-labyrinth with arcades of rose bushes and cypresses. In 1951, under the direction of the architect Prieto Moreno, this was extended with an interpretation of an Islamic garden, with a water channel in cruciform, passageways and cypress masked walls, as well as a pergola with views of the Alhambra and the city. Finally, in 1952 it was completed with an amphitheatre built specially for the International Festival of Music and Dance of Granada, which has been celebrated there each summer since then.

Palacio del Generalife

▼ Portal and entrance patio of the Generalife with the rustic look to be expected, irrespective of its palace status, of a working estate

The entrance to the Generalife buildings presents a curious duality. On the one hand, its external appearance with a rustic portal, concords more with its rural character of farm-

◄ The entrance to the residential part of the Generalife is by these steps and small doorway (background) which preserves in the lintel, a delicate decoration of tiling with the tradition key symbol

► Patio de la Acequia. The central space in the Palacio del Generalife, cruciform in plan and with the Acequia Real running down its length

estate than palace precinct; on the other, the succession of two patios at different levels, with passages before, clearly fits the pattern of access to the Alhambra royal palaces.

The first of these has the modern name **Patio del Descabalgamiento** ('dismounting') after the benches here used for that purpose. It has two lateral rooms, perhaps used by the stableboys. The gate has a certain richness and the impression of a royal entrance is given by the traditional hand and key symbols on the keystone of the arch, the meaning of which has already been explained. A staircase leads up from here and passes, on both sides, benches for the guard. A little room on the upper floor with a window would certainly also have been part of security and control measures.

The second patio, on a higher level and remodelled, used to be surrounded by galleries with arches along each side except the middle one, through which one climbs to the interior of the palace.

162 The entrance to the palace, properly speaking, is through a small door, now half covered with vegetation,

with elements of marble and a tiled lintel; in the middle of which is the key motif, repeated yet again. And finally, another steep and narrow staircase leads into the residential quarters.

Patio de la Acequia

Also known since ancient times as 'Patio de la Ría', this is a narrow elongated space down the middle of which runs a water channel, the **Acequia Real** or Royal Conduit, the **163** principal artery of the hydraulic system in the complex. Its original layout was cruciform, similar to the **Palace of the Lions**, with four elongated octagonal parterres. The famous criss-cross water jets have been an inspiration throughout the world, but were installed only in the 19th century and at a higher level. The archaeological excavations of 1958 revealed the original scheme underneath with twelve spouts.

Being once completely enclosed, the patio used to have an intimacy lost with later alterations. Apart from porticoed pavilions on the short sides, there were also dwellings with upper and ground floors, but on the east side only; these were badly damaged by the fire in 1958 which resulted in the aforementioned excavations.

► The western wall was originally closed to the exterior, the present arcaded gallery was built in times of the Catholic Monarchs, but considerable lowered, as can be seen from the remains of the old building at each end

▼ Interior of the Mirador de la Acequia, the only original opening from the Patio, with views of the Alhambra and the lower city of Granada

El Mirador

The **Patio de la Acequia** was conceived (except for a small mirador or gazebo on the western side) as an inward-looking garden. All this side would originally have been closed in by a tall wall which was lowered in Christian times, as the remaining portions at each end show. At the same time it was opened to the landscape as a sort of *belvedere* and so lost, as has been said, its intimate character. This was done by building a narrow gallery open to the patio through arches which have the arms and emblems of the Catholic Monarchs **165** painted on the soffits.

The central mirador, the only original opening, preserves in the interior, stucco decoration dating from the time of sultan Ismail I (1314-1325). When some of this was removed to the **Alhambra Museum**, it became evident that it had been put up on top of other plasterwork

◀ The interior decoration of the Mirador shows the interesting superimposition of stucco of different times, to be exact of Muhammad III and Ismail I

▼ The portico of the north gallery of the Patio de la Acequia, by J. C. Murphy (1815)

of the time of Muhammad III (1302-1309).

Sala Regia

At the head of the **Patio de la Acequia** is, as is customary, the **Sala Regia** ('Royal Hall'). Before it, and also traditional, is an arcaded gallery of five arches and with alco-

ves at each end. The central arch is very much wider in proportion to the rest and this is in order to frame the triple-arch entrance to the hall behind. The stucco, the niches and the beautiful capitals with mocárabes, stand out once more as protagonistic features. In the same way the distribution of the interior follows the usual pattern, with lateral alcoves framed by arches. Also notable is the projecting cornice of mocárabes just below the base of the wooden ceiling.

In 1494, the Catholic Monarchs added an upper floor

with a gallery open to both the patio and the exterior. This disfigured the Nasrid building, especially a small pavilion above the portico, which must have been similar to the one in the **Palacio del Partal**, which is also topped by a tower connected to the gallery.

▲ An image of the Patio de la Acequia with the pavilion in the background, painted at the begining of the 20th century by a great Granadine watercolourist, Isidoro Marín

On the opposite front there would have been a similar arrangement, but it has been much altered. At ground level it had a portico of five arches. Yusuf III (1408-1417) had an upper floor added with a room from which projects a mirador, remodelled in 1950.

Torre de Ismaíl

In commemoration of the victory of Nasrid troops over

▲ Detail of one of the beautiful capitals with mocárabes in the northern portico of the Generalife

the Castilians in the battle of the Vega or of Sierra Elvira (1319), Ismaíl I (1314-1325) modified the original arrangement of the **Sala Regia**, adding on the principal axis a tower, with a room inside, which is similar to its sisters in the Alhambra. The inside of this tower, decorated with stucco, affords one of the best views of the Alhambra, the city, the Albaycín and the Sacromonte.

The epigraphy which appears on the panel above the triple-arch entrance, is a poem attributed to Ibn al Yayyab (1274-1349) which alludes to warriors of bygone times:

'Alcázar without equal in perfection and beauty on which shines the grandeur of the sultan. / While the generous **169** clouds throw down their rain, its charms gleam and its light glows. / The craftsman's hands worked here the brocade of its walls which seem as flowers of the garden. / Its dais reminds us of a bride adorned with radiant beauty in the nuptual procession. / The singular nature of its dignity is such that watching over it steadfastly is Allah's sultan, / Abu-l-Walid, the pious, the best of the select line of the sultans of Qahtan / and worthy emulator of his pure-blooded ancestors, defenders of the best scion of Adnan, / who so cared for it that in it he renewed / the beautiful craftsmanship as well as its mansions, / in the year of the clamorous triumph of Islam, which in truth has always been a sign of our faith. / May it always be inhabited by Fortune eternal, encompassed by light and the shadow of peace!' (from Sp. trans. by D. CABANELAS, 1984).

◄ Interior of the Torre de Ismail, built for this sultan to commemorate his victory in the Battle of the Vega in 1319

▲ The Patio del Ciprés de la Sultana, scene of legends and one of the most romantic places in the Generalife, as witnessed in this oil painting of 1910 by Joaquín Sorolla.

Patio del Ciprés de la Sultana

Through the lateral alcove of the **Sala Regia** climbs a short staircase to the **Patio del Ciprés de la Sultana** ('of the sultana's cypress') so called for supposedly being the scene of amorous legends set around the tree and described by Ginés Pérez de Hita in his romance of 1595. The building, with portico, dates from 1584; before it is an intimate patio-garden in baroque taste. The palace bath originally covered the whole of this site, but there are no remains apparent except for the entrance of water flowing in the conduit which served **171** it, seen cascading here in a hole in the side wall.

In the middle is a pool with a smaller fountain, added in the 19th century, on top. The whole is ringed by water spouts which freshen the air, something that particularly impressed Andrea Navaggiero, the Venetian ambassador, when he came here in 1526.

▲ Access to the highest part of the Generalife is by this famous Water Stairway, a survivor from the earlier gardens, although much altered. The water rushing down the channels in the side walls is supplied by the sultan's conduit

A small door in the south side of
the patio leads back to the **Patio de la Acequia** and the way out. If time is available and staircases no problem,

the **Upper Gardens** may now be visited by taking the exit opposite the portico.

Upper Gardens and Water Stairway

The **Upper Gardens** are reached via the **Staircase of the Lions**, given its name by the two ceramic figures which crown the portal. In appearance the gardens are more like a 19th century Granadine carmen than an Islamic country estate. They are divided into terraces, dominating the rest of the Generalife at its highest point and so enjoying excellent views.

Small fountains playing between parterres of box, the magnolias, the sequoias and a thoughtful mixture of deciduous trees, make the whole a delightful romantic botanic-garden.

The way out from here is at the end of the garden and through the **Postigo de los Carneros**. Those wishing to continue the visit should now climb, under a pergola of laurel, the **Water Stairway**.

This stairway may have originally led to an oratory (see below) and might therefore have been designed bearing in mind the ablutions required of Muslims before prayer. The stairway is broken by three landings in the middle of each of which are round basins from which, originally, led runnels, now lost. The water channels in the top of the parapets on either side of the stairway are made with upside-down roof tiles and carry a continuous flow of water from the **Acequia Real**.

The poet Juan Ramón Jiménez, stunned by the place, left his impressions: ' ... I heard that music of the water more and more yet at the same time less; less **173** because it was no longer an intimate of mine; the water

was my blood, my life and I heard that the music of my life and blood was the running water'.

▲ This lithograph by A. Guesdon shows the privileged position of the Romantic Mirador in relation to the Generalife estate, the Alhambra and the city of Granada

Mirador Romántico

The **Water stairway** leads to the highest part of the Generalife. On this privileged spot an estate administrator, don Jaime Traverso, built in 1836, a **Romantic Mirador** or belvedere in neo-gothic style. It is very much in the taste of the day, but out of place here, and possibly 174 destroyed an Islamic oratory which some authorities claim was here.

Complementary Open Spaces

Leaving the **Upper Gardens** by the **Postigo de los Carneros** a short descent leads to the **Casa de los Amigos** ('of the Friends') which is the remains of a buil-

▼ The end of the itinerary through the Generalife is along the Oleander Walk, a romantic path on top of one of the dividing walls of the estate

▲ Alongside the Palacio del Generalife are remains of a building known as the Casa de los Amigos ('friends') corresponding as it does to the description of such a lodge for guests and friends found in a 14th century Arabic treatise on the management of a working estate like the Generalife

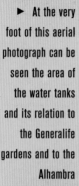

ding complemetary to the Islamic palace. From here starts another celebrated part of the monument, the long **Oleander Walk**, which runs atop a wall separating the gardens and which is entirely covered by a **176** vault of oleander. At the end it joins up with the **Cypress Walk**.

Mid-way along the **Oleander Walk** is the entrance to the Water Itinery which is followed by guided tours at special times.

From the **Cypress Walk** one can enter the precinct of the Alhambra crossing over a modern bridge, or leave the Generalife alongside the **Entrance Pavilion**.

The Environs
of the Alhambra

Apart from visits to the Alhambra monument, it is also possible to visit other complementary areas within the whole complex and which have been arranged as leisurely walks.

The Vermilion Towers

▲ The Vermilion Towers were one of many defensive and observation towers and are directly connected to the Alcazaba of the Alhambra by a long wall

The original building of the **Vermilion Towers** must have belonged to a chain of watch towers placed on strategic heights around the Vega of Granada and which perhaps, included the first **Alcazaba** of the Alhambra. The nineteenth century historian Manuel Gómez-Moreno González, basing his ideas on Luis de Mármol (1520-1600), dated them to the time of Muhammad I, founder of the Nasrid dynasty, although the fabric of the walls, similar to **178** that of the **Alcazaba**, dates back to the 11th century.

At present the complex comprises three towers, the central

one being taller, and a pronounced bastion for artillery built in Christian times. On the surface of the interior walls can be seen a great number of Islamic tombstones, proof that they were reinforced by the Christians.

From here a visit is recommended to the nearby **Fundación Rodriguez-Acosta**, a singular building which belonged to the painter José María Rodriguez-Acosta (1878-1941) and has lovely gardens and views over the city. It plays host to the **Fundación Gómez-Moreno**, the interesting museum and archive of this family of local historians. Eastwards from here and passed the Alhambra Palace Hotel, is the **Paseo de los Mártires** and from here visits are recommended to the **Manuel de Falla Auditorium**, designed by the architect García de Paredes and built in 1978 alongside the **Casa-Museo Manuel de Falla** which, apart from the house itself, includes the personal effects and archive of the famous composer from Cadiz.

Up at the end is the council owned **Carmen de los Mártires** ('of the Martyrs') a nineteenth century romantic villa with magnificent views and gardens open to the public. The villa is used for official receptions.

Parque de los Alijares y Cerro del Aire

The construction of the new approaches to the Alhambra **179** has made the recuperation of a wide, open, public space of

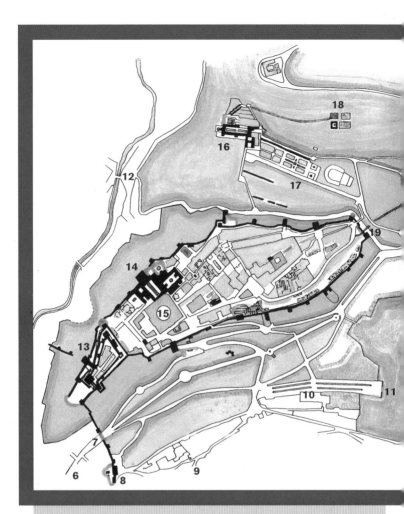

▲ General plan of the whole Monument of the Alhambra and environs: 1. Entrance Pavilion (tickets, lavatories); 2. New approach road; 3. Parque del Cerro del Aire; 4. Parque de los Alijares; 5. Entrance to car park; 6. Cuesta de Gomérez, traditional way up from the city; 7. Puerta de las Granadas; 8. Vermilion Towers ; 9. Pedestrian access by the Cuesta through the Realejo quarter; 10. The Manuel de Falla Auditorium, Museum and Cultural Centre; 11. Carmen de los Mártires; 12. Cuesta del Rey Chico, pedestrian route connecting the Alhambra with the Albayzín and the Sacromonte; 13. Alcazaba;

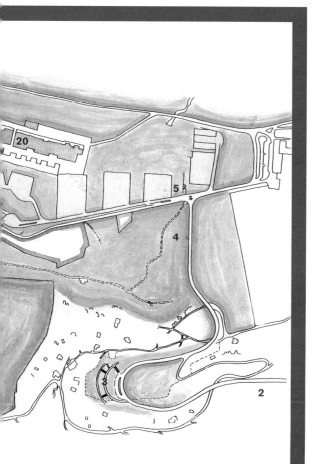

14. Nasrid Palaces; 15. Charles V Palace; 16. Generalife;17. Vegetable Gardens, the New Gardens and the Generalife amphitheatre; 18. Water tanks and Water Itinerary;
19. Connecting bridge between the Alhambra and the Generalife;
20. Archive, library, workshops and warehouses of the Alhambra.

Nasrid buildings ■
Christian buildings □
Archaeological zones
 within the walls ■
Water works ■
Open spaces, gardens,
 woods etc. ■

rural character possible. It is situated in what was an important estate belonging to the sultans called **Parque de los Alijares**. It contains several plots of scrubland, a recovered olive grove as well as the city cemetary and a network of footpaths with benches and look-outs over the Genil valley, the north-east side of Sierra Nevada and the western limits of Granada and includes approximately 115 hectares.

Parque Periurbano de la Dehesa del Generalife

In 1995 an area of 450 hectares around the Alhambra Monument Complex was declared **Parque Periurbano** (approx: Green-belt Land) and was included in the list of protected nature sites in Andalusia. Apart from its character as a rural park and nature reserve, it includes hiking routes, sporting facilities in the **Llano del Perdiz**, and archaeological sites such as the Cerro del Sol, Dar al-Arusa, la **Silla del Moro**, el Aljibe de la Lluvia and the Albercón del Negro.

▶ 1. The 'Paved Cuesta' with a devotional cross of 1599 and the 'Fountain of the Poplars'; 2. Puerta de Bib-Rambla (14th century); 3. Monument of 1921 commemorating the Granadine man of letters Angel Ganivet; 4. Cross set up in 1641 by the Marqués de Mondéjar; 5. The Manuel de Falla Auditorium with the Cadiz composer's house-museum in front; 6. The cross of 1901 commemorating the Christian captives; 7. Carmen de los Mártires; 8. Remains of part of the ingenious Nasrid hydraulic system, known as the 'Albercón del Negro' ('Black Man's Tank'); 9. Aljibe de la Lluvia ('Rainwater Cistern') in the Cerro del Sol; 10. Sundial in the 'Llano de la Perdiz' of the Parque Periurbano of the Generalife; 11. Archaeological remains of a Nasrid palace, 'Dar al-Arusa', in the Cerro del Sol; 12. Sunset from the viewpoint known as the 'Silla del Moro' ('the Moor's Seat'); 13. Part of the Generalife estate and the deep valley of the river Darro from the Sacromonte Abbey; 14. Carpark and new approach roads to the Alhambra; 15. Viewpoint in the Parque de los Alijares; 16. El Cerro del Aire, from los Alijares.

Nasrid Dynasty
(1237-1492)

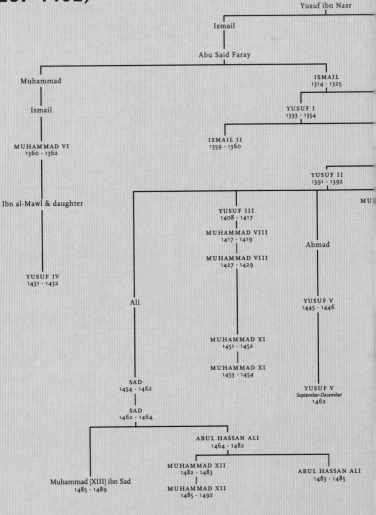

Yusuf ibn Nasr

Ismail

Abu Said Faray

Muhammad

ISMAIL
1314 - 1325

Ismail

YUSUF I
1333 - 1354

MUHAMMAD VI
1360 - 1362

ISMAIL II
1359 - 1360

YUSUF II
1391 - 1392

Ibn al-Mawl & daughter

MU

YUSUF III
1408 - 1417

MUHAMMAD VIII
1417 - 1419

Ahmad

MUHAMMAD VIII
1427 - 1429

YUSUF IV
1431 - 1432

Alí

YUSUF V
1445 - 1446

MUHAMMAD XI
1451 - 1452

MUHAMMAD XI
1453 - 1454

SAD
1454 - 1462

YUSUF V
September-December
1462

SAD
1462 - 1464

ABUL HASSAN ALI
1464 - 1482

MUHAMMAD XII
1482 - 1483

ABUL HASSAN ALI
1483 - 1485

Muhammad [XIII] ibn Sad
1485 - 1489

MUHAMMAD XII
1485 - 1492

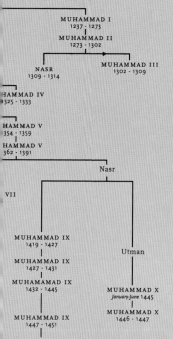

MUHAMMAD I
1237 - 1273

MUHAMMAD II
1273 - 1302

NASR
1309 - 1314

MUHAMMAD III
1302 - 1309

HAMMAD IV
1325 - 1333

HAMMAD V
354 - 1359

HAMMAD V
362 - 1391

Nasr

VII

MUHAMMAD IX
1419 - 1427

MUHAMMAD IX
1427 - 1431

MUHAMAMAD IX
1432 - 1445

MUHAMMAD IX
1447 - 1451

MUHAMMAD IX
1452 - 1453

Utman

MUHAMMAD X
January-June 1445

MUHAMMAD X
1446 - 1447

Regnal names, titles and nicknames
of some granadine sultans

ABUL HASSAN	*Muley Hacem*	MUHAMMAD IX	*el Zurdo*
ISMAIL I	*Abu-l-Walid*	MUHAMMAD X	*el Cojo*
MUHAMMAD I	*al-Galib billah*	MUHAMMAD XI	*el Chiquito*
MUHAMMAD II	*al-Fagih*	MUHAMMAD XII	*Boabdil*
MUHAMMAD III	*al-Majlu*	MUHAMMAD (XIII)	*el Zagal*
MUHAMMAD V	*al-Gani billah*	SAAD	*Ciriza o Muley Zad*
MUHAMMAD VI	*el Bermejo*	YUSUF I	*Abu-l-Hayyay*
MUHAMMAD VII	*al-Mustaín billah*	YUSUF IV	*Abenalmao*
MUHAMMAD VIII	*el Pequeño*	YUSUF V	*Aben Ismael*

Christian sovereigns contemporaneous with the Nasrids

Kingdom of Castille & Leon

FERNANDO III (1217/1229-1252)
ALFONSO X (1252-1284)
SANCHO IV (1284-1295)
FERNANDO IV (1295-1314)
ALFONSO XI (1314-1350)
PEDRO I (1350-1369)
ENRIQUE II (1369-1379)
JUAN I (1379-1390)
ENRIQUE III (1390-1406)
JUAN II (1406-1454)
ISABEL I (1454-1504)

Kingdom of Aragon

JAIME I (1213-1276)
PEDRO III (1276-1285)
ALFONSO III (1285-1291)
JAIME II (1291-1327)
ALFONSO IV (1327-1336)
PEDRO IV (1336-1387)
JUAN I (1387-1395)
MARTIN I (1395-1410)
INTERREGNUM (1410-1412)
FERNANDO I (1412-1416)
ALFONSO V (1416-1458)
JUAN II (1458-1479)
FERNANDO II (1479-1516)

Glossary

This is a condensed version of the glossary in the Spanish version of this book and includes only those words appearing in the English text which may cause difficulty. The original should be consulted by those seeking a fuller understanding of the Spanish and Arabic terminology used in describing the Alhambra.

Acequia: water conduit or channel.

Adarve: a walkway with parapet or battlements, on top of a wall or fortress.

Ajimez: overhanging wooden balcony with celosias.

Alcázar: (Ar. al-qasr), a fortified palace.

Alcazaba: (Ar. al-qasaba), a fortress; in the Alhambra a fortified town in miniature.

Alcove: (Ar. al-qubba) alcove; but in Islamic terms the recess with cushions where the day would be spent; at night a bed.

Algorfa: an upper storey of one room.

Aljibe: a cistern or water tank as an architectural element, usually underground.

Arrocabe: a wooden frieze or panel in the upper part of the wall.

Ataurique: decoration with vegetal motifs.

Barbican: an outwork or detached feature of a fortress sometimes with a tower and planned to protect the main gate.

Bastion: low fortification projecting from the main walls, usually semi-circular in plan.

Capital: the carved top of a column or pilaster.

Carmen: in Granada, a villa with formal and vegetable gardens.

Catholic Monarchs: papal title conferred on Ferdinand and Isabella (1474-1504), the conquerors of Granada.

Celosias: (approx: Jalousie) a lattice screen for windows or other openings made of wood or plaster which filters the light and lets see without being seen.

Corbel: a support of stone or wood projecting from an outside wall.

Cornice: a projecting horizontal feature with moulding running around the wall just below the ceiling.

Cuerda seca: a technique which gives the effect of mosaic tiling but does not use separate ceramic chips, instead different coloured glazes are separated by a thin line to give the geometric pattern.

Cuesta: a street or path climbing a hill.

Cufic: a type of arabic script characterised by its geometrical and rectilinear appearance which, when expanded into texts can become ingenious and decorative compositions.

Cursive: a rounded, flowing script based on handwriting.

Curtain wall: a length of exterior wall between towers.

Cupola: a semi-spherical or conical ceiling over a square, polygonal, circular or elliptical room.

Dado: lower few feet of the wall when the surface is decorated.

Epigraphy: of inscriptions collectively in a building or structural feature. Also the science dedicated to the study of inscriptions.

Frieze: a horizontal broad band of decoration.

Hypocaust: a room in a bath heated from below by hot air.

Jambs: side posts of a doorway or window.

Keystone: the central wedge-shaped stone in an arch.

Lantern: where the ceiling or dome is extended upwards with a turret containing windows to let in natural light.

Lazo: complex geometrical compositions in tiling, wood or plaster based on 6, 8 or 12 pointed stars and expanding infinitely.

Lintel: a piece of wood or stone

laid horizontally over a dooway or window opening.

Medina: a town; in the Alhambra the upper ward containing houses, shops and workshops.

Mihrab: a niche in the qibla of a mosque, pinpointing the direction of Mecca.

Mirador: a belvedere or gazebo; pavilion with views.

Mocárabes: stalactite-like decoration used for vaults, arches and cornices etc. and made by joining together tiny prisms of plaster or wood to give a honeycomb effect.

Morisco: name given to the Muslim community remaining in Granada after the Christian conquest.

Mullion: vertical bar or column dividing the lights in a window; a double window.

Nasrid: The dynasty ruling in Granada from 1238-1492.

Paseo: promenade or avenue for strolling.

Patronato de la Alhambra y Generalife: the governing body which administers the whole monument.

Portal: the main doorway, often richly decorated, in any important building.

Portico: a roofed arcade or gallery with columns.

Qalahurra: a military tower with a royal dwelling inside.

Qibla: the wall in a mosque that indicates the direction of Mecca.

Qur'an: Koran (lit: 'recitation'), the Holy Revelation of Islam.

Rauda: cemetery or pantheon and Islamic garden.

Rusticated: when great blocks of stone, with chips picked out of the surface, are used in a façade to give the impression of great strength.

Secano: lit. un-irrigated land; scrub-, wasteland.

Sebka: decorative rhomboid or lobular elements in a panel.

Sino: the central piece in a design usually a star; symbolically fortune or luck.

Soffit: intrados; the inside or underside curved surface of an arch, between the two faces.

Spandrel: the triangular space between the outer curve of an arch and its enclosing rectangular frame.

Squinch: the arch built across the upper angles of a square room to support a dome or cupola.

Stucco: a facing of plaster with designs and decorations in low relief.

Sura: a chapter of the Qur'an; also a council of ministers.

Taifa: lit. 'of a party or group':

referring to the petty kingdoms established after the fall of the cordoban caliphate at the end of the 11th century.

Vault: a rounded, arched ceiling.

Zirid: dynasty ruling the taifa kingdom of Granada (1013-1090).

Bibliography

ARIÉ, R., *El Reino nasrí de Granada*. Madrid, 1992. ■ BERMÚDEZ PAREJA, J., *La Alhambra. Generalife y Torres*. Florencia-Granada, 1969; —, *Pinturas sobre piel en la Alhambra de Granada*. Granada, 1987. ■ CABANELAS RODRÍGUEZ, ofm., D., *Literatura, Arte y Religión en los Palacios de la Alhambra*. Granada, 1984; — *El techo del Salón de Comares en la Alhambra*. Granada, 1988. ■ CABANELAS RODRÍGUEZ, ofm., D. y FERNÁNDEZ PUERTAS, A., «Inscripciones poéticas del Partal y de la Fachada de Comares» en *Cuadernos de la Alhambra*, Granada, 10-11 (1974-75); —, «El poema de la Fuente de los Leones» en *Cuadernos...* 15-17 (1979-81); —,«Los poemas de las tacas del arco de acceso a la Sala de la Barca» en *Cuadernos...* 19-20 (1983-84). ■ *Cuadernos de la Alhambra*, Granada, volumen I (1965) a volúmenes 33-34 (1997-1998). ■ EGUARAS IBÁÑEZ, J., *Ibn Luyun. Tratado de Agricultura*. Granada, 1988. ■ FERNÁNDEZ PUERTAS, A., *La fachada del Palacio de Comares. The Facade of the Palace of Comares*. Granada, 1980; —, *The Alhambra*. Londres, 1997. ■ FAKHRY, M. (trans.), *The Qur'an*. London, 1997. ■ GALERA ANDREU, P., *La imagen romántica de la Alhambra*. Madrid, 1992. ■ GALLEGO Y BURÍN, A., *La Alhambra*. Granada, 1963. ■ GARCÍA GÓMEZ, E., *Ibn Zamrak. El Poeta de la Alhambra*. Granada, 1975; —, *Poemas árabes en los muros y fuentes de la Alhambra*. Madrid, 1985; —, *Foco de antigua luz sobre la Alhambra*. Madrid, 1988. ■ GÓMEZ MORENO, M., *Guía de Granada*. Granada,1892. ■ GRABAR, O., *The Alhambra*. London, 1978. ■ IRVING, W., *Tales of the Alhambra*. many eds. from 1832. ■ JONES, O., *Plans, Elevations, Sections and Details from the Alhambra*. 2 vols. London, 1842-1845. ■ LADERO QUESADA, M.A., *Granada. Historia de un País Islámico (1232-1571)*. 3ª ed. Madrid, 1989. ■ NYKL, A.R. «Inscripciones Árabes de la Alhambra y del Generalife» en *Al-Andalus*, IV, Madrid-Granada, 1936-1939 ■ RUBIERA MATA, Mª.J., *Ibn al-Yayyab. El otro poeta de la Alhambra*. Granada, 1994. ■ TORRES BALBÁS, L., *La Alhambra y el Generalife de Granada*. Madrid, 1952. ■ VIÑES MILLET, C., *La Alhambra de Granada. Tres siglos de Historia*. Córdoba, 1982. ■ VV AA, *El Palacio de Carlos V. Un siglo para la recuperación de un Monumento*. Granada, 1995; —. *Les jardins de l'Islam. Islamic Gardens*. Granada, 1976.